Raising Teenagers Hassle Free

by
Bob Smith

Harrison House
Tulsa, Oklahoma

Raising Teenagers Hassle Free
ISBN 0-89274-752-8
Copyright © 1990 by Robert B. Smith Jr.
P. O. Box 98800
Seattle, Washington 98198

Published by Harrison House, Inc.
P. O. Box 35035
Tulsa, Oklahoma 74153

Dedication

This book is dedicated to my wife Judi. As a twenty-year-old recently saved newly-wed, she was aware of the desperate need she and I had to learn how to be parents before we had any children. Her diligence in learning and putting into action the godly child-rearing principles she found in the Bible taught as well as inspired me to also do my best. To a large extent, this book is a compilation of what I learned from her.

Contents

Preface   7
 1 Regulated Independence   11
 2 Don't Blame It All on Parents!   19
 3 Setting Standards on Controversial Subjects   25
 4 Flexible and Inflexible Standards   31
 5 Fashions   41
 6 Media   51
 7 Grades   55
 8 Friends   59
 9 Church Attendance   67
10 Curfews   71
11 Chores   73
12 Allowance   77
13 Dating   81
14 Determining Readiness for Dating   91
15 Discipline Is Correction   101
16 Ways of Disciplining   111
Epilogue   121

Preface

I believe my life's work with teenagers is a selfish occupation, because it must be the most entertaining and inspiring work there is! No age group displays more imagination, emotion, enthusiasm, or wildly creative behavior than teenagers. No group challenges the integrity of belief systems and lifestyles more than teenagers. No group can create more chaos and turmoil than teenagers. No human being is more willing to risk everything for a valued cause than a teenager. Teenagers are great, wonderful, stimulating, challenging, and incredibly volatile. The fun never ends!

In just one day, I may hear of the extremes of teenage experience: great stories of a missions trip to El Salvador, fierce battles with siblings, suicide attempts, the joy of bringing someone else to Christ, the very emotional break-up of a boy and girl, and deep, introspective questions.

Those questions are what I call *the whys:*

"Why am I alive in this time and in this place?"

"Why are so many people dying in the world seemingly for no good reason?"

"Why can't I see God?"

"Why can't my parents love one another?"

"What is happening to my body?"

"Why doesn't anybody like me?"

All of these things can happen during a typical day in the life of a teenager. With the proper attitude and a lot of education, these years can be a rewarding and fulfilling time for teens and for parents. But with the wrong attitudes and the wrong knowledge, or information, these years can be "hell on earth" for both groups.

The greatest indicator of an individual's happiness as an adult is the quality of the peer and family relationships during adolescence. Unfortunately, many parents regard adolescence as a sort of "disease" their child sooner or later will catch. They think everything would be great if only they could send their child to a hospital until he, or she, is cured! Even Christian parents who ordinarily live by the Bible get caught in this kind of thinking.

As a youth pastor, I often see this attitude in parents. Society in general has promoted the attitude that teenagers are rebellious and troublesome. Most people believe that if a teen is left to his own devices, he or she will become involved with drugs, get pregnant, or get into some other kind of mischief. Too often this is the prevailing attitude in most homes — but it is the wrong attitude.

In reality, adolescence is simply a transition period everyone experiences while developing from a child into an adult. It is a unique time, because the person is no longer a child but not yet an adult.

Do you still have vivid memories of your teenage years? That was an important time when major decisions were made that affected the rest of your life.

Parents need to realize how important this period of time is, in order to help their teen become the happy, productive, loving person they desire. Too often, however, parents expect their teen to act like an adult, but they treat him like a child. If he makes a mistake, the parent feels he should have known better, although they have not given him the opportunity to learn through having responsibilities and some freedom to make his own decisions.

The proper way to deal with a teen is to treat him like an adult but expect him to act like a child. Give him responsibilities and *some* independence, but know that he is going to be childish and irresponsible at times. A teen will challenge instructions, make mistakes, forget to call home, and in general, act irresponsibly. However, a parent still needs to *give* him responsibilities, respect his dignity, and treat him as an adult.

Take a look at yourself, for example, if you have a teenager in your home. Do you get mad when he exhibits childish behavior, yet also act childish on occasion?

Let's look at what the Bible says about treating young people as adults.

It is good for a man that he bear the yoke in his youth.
Lamentations 3:27

Bearing the yoke means being responsible. The prophet Jeremiah was saying in this verse that it is *good* for a young man to receive responsibility when he is very young. He should be responsible for the way he acts in school, for his grades, his chores, and his participation in church. He should be given responsibilities and be expected to live up to them, yet not condemned when he does not. Make your expectations of his behavior reasonable and in line with what you know of his maturity.

And, ye fathers, provoke not your children to wrath; but bring them up in the nurture and admonition of the Lord.
Ephesians 6:4

Train up a child in the way he should go: and when he is old, he will not depart from it.
Proverbs 22:6

As a parent, you are responsible for training your teenager in the nurture and admonition of the Lord while he is under your roof. This is your most important responsibility. You should lovingly and caringly deal with his wrong behavior and point the way for him to go.

Adolescence can be a scary time as a teen learns to make decisions for himself. Sometimes life will get to be a little too much for him, and the childishness which is still there will surface. He may cry or want his mother, although he may be seventeen years old. He may seem "too big" to act like that, but at the moment, he feels insecure and like a little child. He is afraid and just wants to cry.

That is the time a parent needs to comfort him and let him know everything is safe and secure. A parent needs to motivate teens, care for them, and love them when they act irresponsibly. The important thing is to deal appropriately and responsibly with their behavior, whatever that may be.

1

Regulated Independence

The key to successfully training a teenager is the use of what I call "regulated independence." That may sound contradictory. How can there be independence and regulation at the same time? It is possible, and in fact, that is the way independence should begin.

A teen should gradually acquire more and more responsibility for his life over the years. Give him more independence based on how well he handles each new responsibility.

You might compare this with a situation among nations. If a colony decides it wants to become independent, a wise "mother country" does not immediately pull out and leave the colonists on their own. Usually, they are not prepared to deal with political, military, and economic matters without being trained to take over. Left without counsel and oversight, the newly independent colony would be vulnerable to all kinds of serious problems because of lack of knowledge about business, government, taxation, and defense matters. Independence should be granted, and received, on a regulated, orderly basis.

The same principle applies to rearing children. A teenager should receive his independence and privileges on a regulated basis according to how well he handles his responsibilities.

The "fruit" most parents see in their teens' lives is the result of the training and love they have given them in the past. However, often parents are frustrated, depressed, or angry about their teenager's attitude and behavior. Such parents should not be upset with the teenager, because much of this undesirable fruit is a result of the parents' own behavior and their training when they were children. "Like begets like."

In my role as youth pastor, I sometimes see parents consistently dealing with their children in a negative way. I just shake my head at what I know will come to pass eventually. I do try to tell these parents in a tactful way that their attitudes and behavior are seeds being planted in their children for the future.

If they are mean to a child, eventually they will receive the same fruit from their teen. What a horrible thought for parents whose teenagers now are involved with drugs, sex, total rebellion, rock and roll music, or even criminal activities!

Fruit Comes From the Heart

The Bible clearly states in Matthew 12:33-35 that the fruit of a person's life is based on the treasures stored up in his heart. Bad fruit is a result of bad treasure, and good fruit is the result of good treasure. The treasure is dependent upon the input each person receives during his formative years. The communications media, the type of people surrounding you, the atmosphere or environment in which you live, all have an effect on the treasure of your heart.

The treasure in the heart of a child is primarily controlled by what each parent subjects his child to. If the environment is loving, caring, and uplifting, with protection from negative input, the treasure obviously will be good. Thank God that if we do not like the fruit in our lives or in those of our children, we can change! We change the fruit by changing the treasure.

Often, a teen will reflect the attitudes his parents have, such as fearfulness or being nervous around people. An adult may put up a better front than a teenager, but underneath the veneer of control, one parent — or perhaps both parents — still struggle with nervousness and tension. Their child just has not learned yet how to hide the way he feels.

Sometimes a parent will see his own weaknesses in the teenager and become upset because he resents those things in himself, or he feels responsible for causing the teen to be like him or her.

Report cards are brought home, and perhaps a parent looks at his son's and explodes, "You are so lazy! Why don't you do better? Why can't you be motivated like your sister?"

It would be well for that parent to examine his own life for "laziness" or indolence, in other words, for how much time he spends watching television and how little he spends helping around the house or doing chores. The report card may reflect a "chip off the old block."

Teenagers tend to take everything to extremes, which can be great in some ways; but in others, this tendency can be devastating. The behavior parents see in their teens is a manifestation of their home training. A teenager's room is a perfect example of this.

If it were possible to go into a high school that does not require much discipline from its students and look into the lockers, some of them would be neat and some a mess. Probably, you would not have to even open some of them to know what state they were in — the smell would tell you as soon as you got near! That "fruit," however, is not the product of the high school's training but of parental training.

If parents do not quickly change their thinking and actions as soon as they begin to see bad fruit of their training coming out, the situation will eventually deteriorate from bad to worse. Many homes break up when children get to this age. Either the parents get divorced, the teen runs away from home, or some other tragedy takes place. The fruit has begun to come to harvest, and the parents do not like it. However, they do not, or do not know how, to change their way of thinking and their own attitudes and behavior. They simply react, which is the worst thing they can do.

Inconsistency Breeds Rebellion

Rebellion in a teen results from parental inconsistency. Parents who say one thing and do another are being hypocritical and are sending their children conflicting signals. Sometimes this manifests as forbidding something one week but allowing it the next. Inconsistency in drawing guidelines and setting standards can be a major cause of rebellion.

It is important for parents to develop a consistent lifestyle, because a teenager has tremendous insight. He can recognize hypocrisy in an instant. Teenagers constantly check to make sure their parents are people of integrity, not just because they want to find something to justify rebellion, but because they are looking and hoping to find truth and stability. Inconsistencies in the people who should be their main source of stability constitute a threat to teenagers' sense of security.

Often, a teenager will end up challenging those inconsistencies by rebellion. At which point, most parents deal with the symptoms and never see the root cause of the problem. This teenager, by his behavior, is simply trying to point out inconsistencies in an effort to bring security and stability back into his life.

As a teenager, I remember wanting to find excuses for my bad behavior. I looked for things wrong about my parents — and I always found them. I would have been much better off if I had not been able to use my parents' behavior to justify my own. So it is the parents' responsibility to examine themselves and to get rid of any inconsistencies so their children can feel secure.

If parents would be open to the Holy Spirit, they would see the solution to their problems with teens begins with themselves. Depression and anger at a teenager's behavior will not help. Those are among the worst emotions to "wallow in."

> **Confess your faults one to another and pray one for another, that ye may be healed. The effectual fervent prayer of a righteous man availeth much.**
>
> **James 5:16**

Parents should *not* get defensive and say, "We haven't been bad parents. Our teenager is really the one responsible for all of this."

That attitude only causes additional family strife. Conversely, the parents should not pile all the blame on themselves and go on "a guilt trip." They must forgive themselves and confess their faults to each other so they can pray for each other.

Guilt only leads to more problems and depression. It is vital for parents to look at the reality of what has occurred and get into prayer in order to be healed, to have their home restored, and their teenager retrained.

John 20:23 applies to everyone:

> **Whose soever sins ye remit, they are remitted unto them; and whose soever sins ye retain, they are retained.**

By retaining sins, we will end up repeating them. For example, it is not enough for parents to realize they have trained a son or daughter incorrectly and to accept responsibility for that child's behavior. Parents need to go on to the next step, which is to repent. Genuine repentance will allow the Lord to release them from the guilt of past sins and mistakes.

Guilt Is Not Repentance

Parents cannot afford to waste time and energy in remorse instead of repentance. Remorse allows depression, anger, and condemnation to enter. Feelings of low self-worth are not going to help deal with the teenager. As long as a parent holds onto the sin through guilt and remorse or through refusal to admit it, the same negative behavior will be repeated again and again.

It is okay to say, "I blew it. I messed up. I did the wrong thing. Either I did not have the knowledge I needed or I was not able to act on what I did know."

Whatever the situation, parents must let go of blame. They cannot go back in time and relive those parts of their lives. They must realize that God is full of mercy and will forgive them, according to First John 1:9:

If we confess our sins, he is faithful and just to forgive us our sins, and to cleanse us from all unrighteousness.

No parent can do irreparable damage to their children, because God's grace is bigger than all their mistakes. God is able to reach a child no matter what the parents have done. Love covers a multitude of sins. (1 Pet. 4:8.) That means that no matter what mistakes parents have made, if they will change and seek God's plan for their lives, the damage that has been done can be turned or mitigated.

True repentance will cause parents to change their own lifestyles and confess their faults to their teens.

They can say, "Son or daughter, I know I am responsible for much of your behavior, because I did not do a very good job of training you. But I am a changed person now. Jesus has made a difference in my life, and I am going to live for Him. I love you so much that I am going to require that you live differently also.

"I cannot change your heart. You must make your own decision about Jesus. However, to live in my house, you will have to abide from now on by the standards of the Word of God. From now on, I am going to be a consistent parent and love you according to the Word of God."

The teenager may not like this. He may rebel. Hey may hate the changes. He may even want to "hit the door" and say, "Adios, Amigos. See you later, Mama!"

But at least he will know his parents love him and are now stable. He will know he can rely on them now for straight answers. When he finally decides he is tired of struggling alone with his problems, he will remember the love and guidance available to him from his parents. Mom and Dad just need to keep communicating this message:

"We love you so much, but we are not going to feel badly about the things we have messed up in the past. We have confessed them, and they are under the blood of Jesus. We cannot change the consequences of those things, but we are free of them, and we are moving on from here. You can too."

Keeping a positive attitude is vitally important for a parent, especially if he or she is a newly converted Christian. Parents who are saved after their children have reached the teenage stage usually have been living a worldly life for a long time. That teenager naturally acts the way he already has been trained.

This can cause parents to feel so badly that they begin misguided efforts to change things overnight. Instead of helping the teen, that may hurt him. His parents say they are Christians now; yet to him, they are not acting in as loving a manner as perhaps they did before. This does not result in a great testimony to the teenager on the benefits of accepting Jesus as Savior and Lord.

The parents' behavior after conversion can be so inconsistent with their past attitudes that the change registers in the teenager as inconsistency, and he resists because he feels insecure.

However, the Word does not place all of the responsibility for a young person's actions and attitudes on the family. In the next chapter, we will see all the blame should not be placed on parents.

2

Don't Blame It
All on Parents!

God had some things to say to the Israelites about child rearing — some tough things. And he held young people responsible for their own actions. His instructions for dealing with a rebellious young person was drastic!

> If a man have a stubborn and rebellious son, which will not obey the voice of his father, or the voice of his mother, and that, when they have chastened him, will not hearken unto them:
>
> Then shall his father and his mother lay hold on him, and bring him out unto the elders of his city, and unto the gate of his place;
>
> And they shall say unto the elders of his city, This our son is stubborn and rebellious, he will not obey our voice; he is a glutton, and a drunkard.
>
> And all the men of his city shall stone him with stones, that he die: so shalt thou put evil away from among you; and all Israel shall hear, and fear.
>
> **Deuteronomy 21:18-21**

Notice one thing: *God did not say to stone the parents as well.* He held the son responsible for his own actions after a certain age. And he did not tell the parents to give that rebellious son a little spanking. No, God knew one rebellious teenager can begin to affect others of his peer group. But I am happy to be under the grace of God provided by the New Covenant rather than under the legalism of the law.

However, even in the New Testament, the Holy Spirit dealt with situations involving people who cause strife. In Romans 16:17: Paul wrote, under the inspiration of the Holy Spirit:

> Now I beseech you, brethren, mark them which cause divisions and offences contrary to the doctrine which ye have learned; and avoid them.

And Paul wrote in Titus 3:10,11:

> Reject a divisive man after the first and second admonition,

> Knowing that such a person is warped and sinning, being self-condemned.

These verses usually are used in connection with people who stir up strife in churches; however, the principle can be applied to anyone who stirs up strife, even a teenager. The principle is: Do not let someone causing strife continue indefinitely. A teen needs to be confronted about his behavior and dealt with decisively.

With love, patience, and authority, the teenager must be brought out of the place of strife into a place of submission. The point I want to make is that, regardless of how incompetent the parents have been in the past, they cannot use guilt as an excuse for not dealing with the behavior of their teenager now. God requires every parent to deal with the behavior of his children.

Guilt will cause a parent to hold his own wrong behavior against his child, particularly when that child gets into the teen years. Some parents like a child when he is being "nice," but that means they do not really like that child. They simply like him for their own sake. He is not causing them problems.

There are parents who do not love their teenagers, because they were not loved as children. They are full of anger and hatred, which pops out all the time. Self-hatred gets projected onto the teenager when he exhibits behavior that has been learned from the parent.

Many times, a teenager feels he is big enough not to take that kind of treatment or attitude any longer. Then he pushes those negative things right back in the parent's face.

Some horrible things can happen in an environment like this. This is the time when a crisis is likely to occur.

This kind of situation does not just occur in the over-crowded areas of big cities or on soap operas. This parent-child confrontations are taking place right in the Church. Many Christian parents are so angry at themselves that, instead of forgiving themselves, they turn these angry feelings against the teenager.

The good news is that there are many families with happy teenagers, families where relationships are positive. Your family may be one of these. If so, thank God. Receive the principles as increased knowledge on good parenting.

For those who can relate to the negative examples I have given, take heart! The effort you are making to change will release the power of God to work in your relationship with your teenager.

Every Reason To Have Hope

My wife and I have experienced the change wrought by the power of God in our own family. Judi and I married immediately after completing a drug rehabilitation program. She was twenty, and I was twenty-two, and we began our family right away.

However, at our young ages and with our negative backgrounds, we made many mistakes rearing our daughter. At that point, we had little knowledge of the Word of God. The one thing we did have going for us was our commitment to learn, grow, and change; a good church in which to learn; and a network of people on whom we could depend for help and advice. Sometimes these people approached us, and we did not even have to ask for help.

Consequently, today we are enjoying the fruit of our labors in the life of our teenage daughter.

There is every reason to have hope.

21

There is every reason to believe that your situation or your child can turn around, if that is what is needed. Take heart! I have seen case after case of families with difficult situations change for the better.

There *is* a price to pay, and that price is: a lot of work. But it will not be in vain. Do not judge by what you see in the immediate future in your teenager. Christians are to walk by faith and not by what they can see.

As a youth pastor, I have had reason to prove this Bible principle over and over. Many times, with teenagers, I must walk by faith. Most teenagers' faces will never reveal what is going on inside. If I had walked by sight, I might have quit being a youth pastor a long time ago!

Parents who become discouraged would do well to claim the promise in Mark 4:26-29, which is that good seed planted *will* in due season bring forth a harvest of good fruit. Parents with a rebellious teenager should take comfort from the fact that his life is not yet over. Their responsibility now is just to continue planting seeds. A teenager may seem to reject his parents' training and guidance, but those seeds will not get rooted out if they are truly planted in him.

If my own parents had walked by sight during my teen years, my outward behavior might have inspired them to commit suicide! I was totally messing up my life. If they had given up then, they would never have seen me change. Looking back, I can only be glad that life is not over at eighteen.

I do realize that it is sometimes easier for me to accept and handle teenagers who act tough, cool, and rebellious in my class at church than it is for their parents. I know how to love them, because I used to be one of them.

It is not as easy for parents to say, "No big deal. I am just going to keep planting the seed, and I believe God is going to work in their lives. I *will* see them change."

But that is exactly what the parents *need* to say. They must stand on the Word of God and continue to work with that teenager.

To develop a right attitude in training and disciplining their teenager, parents must focus primarily on what he needs, not on what they need. The right focus will keep you from getting mad, disgusted, and depressed. Being obsessed by your own feelings will not help you remain stable and supportive.

A teenager needs love, encouragement, consistency, and discipline from his parents. Focusing on his failures will only hinder the parents' ability to strengthen and improve the relationship.

Teenagers Need a Challenge

Another need teenagers have is for a challenge. The more I challenge the teenagers in my youth group, the more they grit their teeth and respond. In my leadership training classes, I really put a challenge to them, and they keep coming back for more. Young people thrive on challenges, because they need motivation.

Parents can motivate their teens by helping them to establish goals and visions in their lives, either by encouragement — "Hey, you *can* do this" — or by pointedly directing them — "You *need* to do this." Sometimes the authoritative approach needs to be used to keep teens growing and moving.

As a junior high student, our daughter got the idea that average grades ("C's") were good, "B's" were very good, but "A's" basically were unattainable by her. At first, we challenged her about his, but her doubts as to her abilities and some laziness kept her from responding to encouragement.

Then we told her, "You are too smart to settle for a 'C'. That is not acceptable. We are going to help you achieve the best of which you are capable."

After a couple of tense years of making demands about homework and sitting down and helping her (which included my taking an algebra class in order to learn what I needed to know to help her), her vision and her expectations for herself were raised. Now she is self-motivated to get the best grades. This would never have happened if we had accepted the level of performance she first established for herself.

3

Setting Standards on Controversial Subjects

Whether a teenager's home atmosphere is peaceful or chaotic depends on how the parents handle controversial subjects. During my teenage years, whenever a crisis arose and was handled wisely, the situation mellowed out and things settled down. When the crisis was handled incorrectly, there was an explosion, and bitterness, division, and strife would take over.

I know from personal experience that how controversial subjects are handled is critical to the atmosphere of the home and to the relationship between parents and teens. It is very important for parents to be prepared for trouble in advance. When the pressure is on full blast, it is very difficult to "get your act together."

First, parents should establish their own personal standards. They must know exactly where they stand on certain issues to avoid jumping from one side of a fence to the other. They should not tell their children to do one thing, while the children see them doing the opposite. That is the inconsistency of which I wrote in chapter one.

> **Then spake Jesus to the multitude, and to his disciples,**
>
> **Saying, The scribes and the Pharisees sit in Moses' seat.**
>
> **All therefore whatsoever they bid you observe, that observe and do; but do not ye after their works: *for they say, and do not.***
>
> **Matthew 23:1-3**

What Jesus was saying is that religious people tell you to do good things, but many times, they do not do those things themselves. So do whatever they say, and do not follow whatever they do. However, in dealing with young people, that old saying of "do as I say and not as I do" is usually considered a bunch of "hogwash" that provokes rebellion.

Parents should get their own priorities and beliefs straightened out before they tell their teenagers how to live. They need to compare what they are asking teenagers to do with what they demand of themselves. If parents would begin to set good examples, about 99 percent of the problems would be eliminated.

Parents Must Be Examples

In Philippians 3:14-17, the Apostle Paul instructed the church at Philippi to follow his example, and that is what every parent should be able to say: "Son, or daughter, be ye followers of us parents."

Teenagers should be able to grow up in their parents' footsteps to achieve a good and godly life. If the parental example is not good, then parents do not have much credibility with their children. Teens can tell when mom and dad are being liars, hypocrites, or phonies no matter how well it is packaged.

When my parents told me one thing but did something else, I discounted everything they said to me and would not obey. Many parents set a bad example, but expect their teenager to be better than they are. But life just does not work that way.

First Timothy 4:12 says:

> Let no man despise they youth; but be thou an example of the believers, in word, in conversation, in charity, in spirit, in faith, in purity.

The word translated *conversation* really means lifestyle; *charity* means love, and *purity* means holy living. Parents are to be examples in all of these things. Verses 13 and 14 continue:

> Till I come, give attendance to reading, to exhortation, to doctrine.

> Neglect not the gift that is in thee, which was given thee by prophecy, with the laying on of the hands of the presbytery.

The word *presbytery* literally means "a group of elders," and in a family, the "elders" are the parents. As soon as a husband and wife become parents — even from the very moment their child is conceived — they have entered the "presbytery."

> Meditate upon these things; give thyself wholly to them; that thy profiting may appear to all.

> Take heed unto thyself, and unto the doctrine; continue in them: for in doing this thou shalt both save thyself and them that hear thee.

> 1 Timothy 4:15,16

Parents need to demonstrate to their teenagers that a complete surrender to the standards of Christian living is something that will bring tremendous benefits to them just as it has to mom and dad.

Measure Everything by the Word

First of all, parents should devote some time to examining their own lives by questioning what attitudes and behaviors they need to change. They need to get involved with the teaching and the will of God. This will help them discover how their thinking and actions agree and disagree with God's Word. That will not only "save" the parents (much trouble and heartache), but also those who hear them — their children.

This is a powerful concept for parents to get hold of, one that will help them win their children for the Lord. If parents will heed this doctrine of the Bible and live godly and holy lives, they will save themselves and also their children.

For this to work, each parent must make a consistent, lifetime commitment. Inconsistency breeds rebellion, as I stressed in the last chapter.

For example, let us say a parent has been going "full-steam ahead" for the Lord for a period of about three months. He has faithfully been going to church, praying and reading his Bible.

Then, all of a sudden, he drops out of church for about two months, returns to watching forty hours of television a week, is depressed, and experiences all kinds of upsets. Now, that is inconsistency.

Another example is a parent who spends three months loving his teenager and believing for the best for him. He encourages the teenager and deals with his behavior as needed. Then, something happens to disrupt the relationship. Perhaps, a parent finds he has too much work to spend time with his children and assumes the children will understand the circumstances.

For the next few weeks, the parent spends all his time on work and forgets about the children, rationalizing that the other parent will take care of them. Parents who fall into the trap of inconsistency will soon find rebellion operating in his home.

When it comes to establishing specific standards, parents, not teenagers, must be in control. Perhaps this seems obvious to some people; however, everyone does not realize how important it is for mom and dad to be the ones who decide what the family's standards will be.

Do Not Expect Too Much

Parents must set the pace in things such as church attendance, prayer, Bible study, and having a godly attitude.

They certainly should not expect more from their children than they do from themselves.

Teenagers should see their parents working daily to improve themselves. Parents should admit it when they are wrong, even to their children. Teens are searching for truth. When they see that their parents value truth, are willing to admit their own faults, and are willing to change their own behavior, teenagers may also realize they need to work on things in themselves.

There are many angry teenagers who believe their parents think they know everything and teenagers do not know anything. Parents need to show their teenagers that mom and dad are not perfect. They do not "have it all together" as yet, and they need to keep growing and changing in their lives as well.

A teen can more easily accept constant correction, instruction, and discipline from his parents if those parents are willing to admit they can be wrong. Once parents and teens get down to common ground, the leadership issue does not become such a big problem. Teenagers will accept leadership when that leadership proves it can be respected.

Standards concerning unacceptable, negative behavior also have to be established by parents, and they should be communicated directly to the family in the form of a "decree." Parents should be very explicit and firm about attitudes and behavior that will not be tolerated.

Parents should not feel they have to justify forbidding something. Either use the Bible to back up your standards, or let teens know God has given parents both the responsibility and authority to rear children to the best of their abilities — and that is just the way it is. You should remember, however, that you must meet or exceed the same standards you set for them.

4

Flexible and
Inflexible Standards

Standards can be categorized as either flexible or inflexible. A flexible standard could concern things such as music, clothes, or hairstyles. The parents' standards on these things may be open to some modifications.

Inflexible standards would be in areas such as drugs, drinking, and sex — no changes, no bending of rules, period!

Parental authority on inflexible standards must be absolutely unquestionable and unchallengeable. Teenagers must know these standards and the discipline they will receive if they fail to comply with them.

Setting inflexible standards requires wisdom and knowledge on the part of parents. If they have any doubts as to what is best, they should ask for input from other knowledgeable people who work with teens, such as youth pastors, youth workers, and teachers.

Flexible standards usually are more difficult to determine without seeking additional advice. Possible sources of help are other parents who are doing a good job of raising their teenagers. If their teenagers are happy and "fired up," find out what their standards are. Which ones are flexible? Where do those parents draw the line? Also, teens with positive attitudes probably would be happy to talk to someone else's parent who was sincerely interested in getting some advice.

Before jumping headlong into setting standards where none have been set before, parents should spend some time meditating on what their goals are for themselves and their family. Also, they should consider all the eventualities that can occur in today's society.

Parents who say, "Why worry about setting standards for problems that will never come up in our home," are definitely operating "in a fog."

The Bible says foolishness is bound in the heart of a child. (Prov. 22:15.) It *will* come out at different times, and parents must be ready to deal with it. But first let young people know ahead of time what discipline will be used.

Following is a pattern for a "policy statement" that might be adopted when a teen is ready to do certain things:

"All new levels of independence and increases in privileges will be determined by the responsibility demonstrated by you on previous levels."

The teen should understand that this "policy" will mean that his recent behavior will have a direct impact on how much freedom he will enjoy. The teenager could then see that most decisions concerning his freedom and his privileges are to be determined by his actions and not by his parents' orders. That means freedom for mom and dad.

Definite Standards Free Parents and Teens

If a teen who has been told this policy exists gets angry at not being allowed more privileges, the parents can refer back to "the policy" and show him how he blew it for himself. They can demonstrate that he was not ready for more freedom because he did not act responsibly with the last freedom he received.

This policy should not be used as a weapon, however.

It is not fair to retain the record of a teenager's past mistakes for an inordinate amount of time or to insist that he behave like an absolute angel before he can have another privilege. Parents must be fair about it. They are not even that hard on themselves, right? However, the policy statement can be a great parenting tool as long as it is used wisely.

This policy, or principle, relates directly to the regulated independence discussed in chapter one. A teen's movement to a higher level of independence will be determined by how he handled things, or how responsible he was, on the previous level. That goes for everything: dating, music, curfews, grades, having a car, and so forth.

When a teen wants to get a driver's license and begin to drive, or when he wants to get involved in athletics, parents should say, "Well, let's look at your past behavior. How are your grades?"

Then the teenager is completely responsible for deciding whether he wants to change the behavior that prevents him from acquiring more privileges. Parents are to help their children attain their goals. Children need help and encouragement from parents. That is how God treats us, His children.

He does not say, "Well, there it is. Make it, or break it."

Matthew 25 contains the parable of the master who distributed different amounts of talents among his servants. The servants then were blessed according to how well they handled the talents. Verse 21 says:

> **His lord said unto him, Well done, thou good and faithful servant; thou hast been faithful over a few things, I will make thee ruler over many things: enter thou into the joy of thy lord.**

Those who were faithful and responsible with the money they had been given were rewarded with even more responsibility. Parents should deal with their teens in the same way.

There is nothing wrong with parents showing teenagers how God deals with people by reading the Bible with him, but the Word should not be used as a club to thump teens over the head. The Bible is for guidance and direction, not judgment and criticism.

Luke 16:10 says:

> He that is faithful in that which is least is faithful also in much: and he that is unjust in the least is unjust also in much.

Teenagers often accuse their parents of unfairness by saying, "You just don't trust me."

The parents need to respond, "Wait a minute! How much I trust you is not the point. We are talking about facts. If you have been irresponsible in a little thing, then you are more than likely to be irresponsible in the big things, and I am not willing to let that happen to you."

Faithfulness in Little Things

Another good scripture for parents to explain to teens is Luke 16:11, which says:

> If therefore ye have not been faithful in the unrighteous mammon, who will commit to your trust the true riches?

If teens are not responsible with their money, how can they handle the true riches that are their mental or spiritual attributes? If they cannot handle money, what in the world will happen to them when they get involved with the flesh? Dating is a good example.

A person's soul is true riches to God. If young people cannot manage their money wisely, how can parents trust them with God's true riches, which are their own lives? Teens are not prepared for that. They can be terribly scarred by any negative relationship, not just sexually immoral ones. Teens are so very vulnerable and can form very strong emotional attachments.

Then there comes the time for turning a young person loose. If he has not been faithful in living up to the standards his parents have set, how can he possibly be expected to establish reasonable standards for himself?

Parents can say, "Son, or daughter, we want to give you some teaching from the Bible. If you are having difficulties following the standards we are giving you, how in the world will you be able to go out into the world, set your own standards, and live according to the Word? You won't be able to.

"In order to have a happy and successful life alone, you must do as you are told now. You must learn to follow our instructions and standards as we set them according to the Word of God. If you refuse, you will have a tough time living on your own."

Drugs, Alcohol, and Music

Standards on drinking and drugs fall into the inflexible category in which no questions or challenges are allowed. I am writing with the assumption that the reader does not believe in the use of either alcohol or drugs.

Most drug users begin the habit because they are not happy with their lives in some way, either they feel unloved, unaccepted, or lonely in their home lives. Others begin to take drugs because their peer group is into drugs. In this case, they become hooked for *fear* of not being accepted and not being part of the crowd. Drugs are temporary, artificial, and dangerous, but for that brief moment, the user feels good.

A high school football coach in our area grew so tired of his players' flirting with drugs and then denying using them that he established a strict and inflexible standard. If his players use drugs or alcohol or are in the presence of them, they are off the team. This eliminates the protest of, "Yeah, I was there, but I didn't do anything." I support the same policy for the family.

There is no room for flexibility on these standards. Leaving an open door will create a lot of problems in the family. If a teenager is involved in drinking or drugs, it is just the tip of the iceberg. There usually are deeper problems going on inside the young person that will require a lot of help.

The lie that "everybody's doing it," that drugs are socially acceptable and perfectly normal, is a lie of the devil. Parents of a teenager involved in drinking and drugs have a serious problem to deal with. The main thing parents should do is seek help immediately for both the teenager and the family. Definitely, they should not compromise their standards by ignoring the situation.

Inflexible standards may cause a terrible upheaval in the home for the time being. It may seem grievous to a teenager that mom and dad are so inflexible about standards concerning alcohol, drugs, and sex. But the real grief would be for that teen to mess up his thinking and his life by being involved in such dangerous behavior.

Teens should be reminded of what Hebrews 12:11 says:

Now no chastening for the present seemeth to be joyous, but grievous: nevertheless afterward it yieldeth the peaceable fruit of righteousness unto them which are exercised thereby.

If there were no other reason for inflexible standards on drinking and drugs, the fact that they are against the law for underage teens would be enough. However, hopefully, Christian parents would forbid their teenagers to participate in drinking and taking drugs even if that was allowed by law. Drinking *is* legal for adults, but Christians should not drink because alcohol is harmful to the body.

Also, alcohol damages a person morally, emotionally, and spiritually. There should be no question that drinking or taking drugs are unacceptable and should be dealt with severely. However, parents should not interpret "severely" to include beating their teens to a pulp! Instead, parents should see their behavior as a red light or an alarm sounding signals of danger ahead. Those signals mean parents need to get the entire family involved with counseling. I will cover more on this topic in later chapters.

Music is another controversial topic with teenagers, and the answer lies in the overall concept of the treasure of the heart and the fruit it produces. The music a person listens to definitely has an effect on the treasure in his heart. Therefore, it is a matter of the quality of fruit a person desires for himself. I believe anything that does not contradict or conflict with the Word of God is not going to produce a negative treasure.

If the lyrics to any music do not violate the following scriptures, I do not see any scriptural mandate to reject any particular *style.* However, if the lyrics or the mood of any song causes a person to think or act in violation of these scriptures, then it is to be rejected regardless of the style, whether it is country-western, rock and roll, or even classical.

> **Casting down imaginations, and every high thing that exalteth itself against the knowledge of God, and bringing into captivity every thought to the obedience of Christ.**
> **2 Corinthians 10:5**

> **Finally, brethren, whatsoever things are true, whatsoever things are honest, whatsoever things are just, whatsoever things are pure, whatsoever things are lovely, whatsoever things are of good report; if there be any virtue, and if there be any praise, think on these things.**
> **Philippians 4:8**

Parents need to follow the same standards required of their teens or else they are being hypocritical. So parents must set the example. Since most secular music is off-limits to the standards of Christian parents, that music should be replaced with some that teenagers can enjoy.

Set Standards by Content, Not Style

When it comes to selecting the kind of Christian music teens will listen to, parents should be flexible. They should not expect their children to have the same musical tastes as their own. Teenagers more than likely will *not* like the same kind of music mom and dad do.

I once thought the only godly music was praise music or hymns. Have my standards changed over the years! I walked out of the first concert I attended by trumpet-player Phil Driscoll. I thought he was negative, worldly, and a rock-and-roller. I was convinced he could not be of God.

Yet, later, I witnessed supernatural events that resulted from his music. I saw a young man healed of deafness as Phil Driscoll was "jamming." He was not quietly singing, "We exalt thee," but blasting away. That teenager was healed while the crowd was dancing and going wild. I could not argue with that kind of fruit, so my standards had to change.

Parents should not just say, "No, you cannot listen to this Christian band or that one."

What if you are wrong? What would happen if your teen listened anyway and saw someone being healed, or even was healed himself? Suppose your teen who wears glasses came home with his eyesight perfectly restored at that band's concert? What could a parent say then?

Find a balance between music that tends to put you to sleep and that which is too raucous for you to accept. Christian songs should have a strong spiritual message.

Also, I would like to point out that, in my opinion, some of the Christian music on the market today is trash — not because of its style or volume, but because of its lack of spiritual depth and because of its contradiction of Biblical doctrine.

There are some churches and some Christian teachers I would not take my youth group to hear because they plant doubt and disbelief about some of the Word which we teach and believe. The situation with Christian musicians is no different. Each song writer or musician has his own doctrinal beliefs, and if their lyrics contradict the Word of God, those songs should be rejected.

A very popular artist recently issued a musically great album, but the predominant message was what a struggle it is to live the Christian life! While I enjoyed the music, I did not listen to the album because the Bible tells me a different message. I do not need to listen to someone not living according to the Word tell me how hard the Christian life is to live.

There is a lot of good Christian music out there that is upbeat and fun. Some parents are not crazy about the style, but this music does motivate teens to praise God and be happy. Also, there is quite a bit of good music available making a statement about our society and Christians' responsibility to do something about it. This music is positive as long as it is conscience-provoking rather than rebellion-provoking.

Musical style, as I have said, rather than musical content, is the place where mom and dad can display some flexibility. Parents should remember that a teenager's musical taste will not mature overnight. He needs some room to be young, to grow, and to change. If he has been a rock fan, he will not get saved and immediately switch over to listening to Sandi Patti.

Teenagers usually do not like the same music as adults, and they certainly like their music louder! Some noise will not hurt them if it causes them to talk about God, praise God, and be involved with the things of God. One thing is certain, musical styles have consistently changed over the centuries, and I doubt there has ever been a generation in which parents and children enjoyed the same kind of music!

One thing that should be promoted is your teenager's involvement in some type of praise and worship in which the presence of the Holy Spirit is manifested. In order to keep moving with God, teenagers need to get involved with music that will create a desire in them to praise and worship God, which will, in turn, usher them into the presence of the Lord.

5

Fashions

The Pharisees once challenged Jesus about his disciples eating food with unwashed hands, which was contrary to the Jewish laws and traditions. According to their legalistic minds, a failure to be physically clean would result in the inner man being defiled.

Jesus, Who was spiritually minded rather than carnally (naturally) minded, confronted them about hypocrisy, and then told his followers:

> And when he had called all the people unto him, he said unto them, Hearken unto me every one of you, and understand:
>
> There is nothing from without a man, that entering into him can defile him: but the things which come out of him, those are they that defile the man.
>
> If any man have ears to hear, let him hear.
>
> And when he was entered into the house from the people, his disciples asked him concerning the parable.
>
> And he saith unto them, Are ye so without understanding also? Do ye not perceive, that whatsoever thing from without entereth into the man, it cannot defile him;
>
> Because it entereth not into his heart, but into the belly, and goeth out into the draught, purging all meats?
>
> And he said, That which cometh out of the man, that defileth the man.
>
> For from within, out of the heart of men, proceed evil thoughts, adulteries, fornications, murders,
>
> Thefts, covetousness, wickedness, deceit, lasciviousness, an evil eye, blasphemy, pride, foolishness:

All these evil things come from within, and defile the man.

Mark 7:14-23

It is very important for parents to establish appropriate standards for the things teenagers can feed into their minds, because it is the content of the heart that makes a person "unclean," or negative. Parents should be aware of the type of information their child is receiving from sources such as television, books, music, and movies.

The style of clothing the young person wears or the food he eats will not defile him, because the outer man and the belly do not make a person unclean, according to the scriptures. Attitudes and ways of thinking is what will harm that son or daughter.

Fashions Do Matter

However, fashions do matter because they reflect the state of the heart. Some Christian teenagers may dress in a questionable manner and not realize it. They do not perceive fashion as conforming to the world. All they know is that this style is what all of their peers are wearing, and in it, they feel comfortable and a part of the crowd.

Other teens might wear the same clothes as a statement of their attitudes. Styles are affected by the latest look of popular secular singers and movie stars, and worldly teenagers want to look and dress just like them because they identify with that hero or heroine's message and beliefs. They know exactly what is going on in the world and know that their clothes' style communicates a spirit of total and utter rebellion. Those are the teens who are harming themselves with inward negative thoughts and attitudes.

Therefore, parents need to evaluate what is going on in that teenager's heart and mind, not what he or she is wearing. Just because a teenager buys a radical jacket loaded with zippers, studs, rhinestones, or whatever the current radical look is, does not mean he is trying to emulate the attitudes and behavior of the entertainer who inspired that look. He may not even know who some of those people are! He just knows these styles are popular, and he likes them.

Two completely different mind sets are involved, and parents need to examine the heart and mind of their teen before they begin to judge and get paranoid about rebellion.

Setting standards can be tricky. Christians should be careful not to go to extremes in either direction — not to be too conservative or too liberal. Some religious traditions developed over the years set incredibly rigid standards of dress, cosmetics, and hair styles. Breaking these "religious" rules could get you branded immoral and a sinner. Women who wore makeup in these churches were called "Jezebels," including those who wore slacks, short sleeves, gold jewelry, or "bobbed" hair. Women could not cut their hair, but on the other hand, must wear it pinned up on their heads — not hanging down their backs.

Those are the same kinds of standards Jesus talked to the Pharisees about: concentrating on the outward appearance and not the inward heart. Legalism and religion are forms of extremely conservative standards. A major problem with these viewpoints is that they get old fast.

Teenagers do not want to be out of date and "stuffy," and neither should parents. Once a person's outlook gets old, it is just a short hop to being dead.

Parents can force their teenagers to conform to a religious and legalistic mold, but that will not guarantee a change on the inside.

The other extreme would be an "anything-goes," wild, loose, rebellious, and worldly attitude toward dress. Living on this fast and unstable track will cause a person to burn out. Both extremes can result in destruction of some kind, but the last alternative is more appealing to a young person.

Standards Should Be Balanced

To be effective, standards must be balanced. Parents should avoid getting stuck at one of the extremes. Naturally, they cannot allow their teenager complete freedom to do whatever he wants, but they *should* consider his opinions to avoid being overly legalistic. Parents who set standards based on their own likes and dislikes will appear narrow-minded and old-fashioned to their teens. This will create a barrier to communications.

Teenagers enjoy parents who are young at heart and full of life. It is possible for mom and dad to be interesting people and still remain godly. Parents should not get in a rut in their lives, their attitudes, and their thinking. They cannot make decisions and set standards for teenagers and expect things never to change.

Most things in life are dynamic, not static. Everyday issues such as fashions, makeup, hairstyles, and music are changing continually. What once was young, alive, and exciting is now legalistic, religious, and old. Standards should be updated on occasion but always within godly boundaries. Romans 12: 1,2 are good scriptures to discuss with young people.

> **I beseech you therefore, brethren, by the mercies of God, that ye present your bodies a living sacrifice, holy, acceptable unto God, which is your reasonable service.**
>
> **And be not conformed to this world: but be ye transformed by the renewing of your mind, that ye may prove what is that good, and acceptable, and perfect, will of God.**

Christians are to look on their bodies as belonging to God. Parents might ask their teen if he thinks he is dressed in a manner holy and acceptable to God. Would he be cool cruising around with Jesus? Would Jesus wear the same styles, listen to the same music, or hang out in the same places? If parents will discuss these issues in an open and supportive manner, the teen will be honest with them, and a good foundation will be laid for future communications.

Not conforming to the world does not mean Christians should look and act like a bunch of "fuddy-duddies." We should not remain with carnal, sinful values and interests, but we need to be alive, fresh, and exciting. Christians should be the ones who set trends and come up with new ideas.

> But the Lord said unto Samuel, Look not on his countenance, or on the height of his stature because I have refused him: for the Lord seeth not as man seeth; for man looketh on the outward appearance, but the Lord looketh on the heart.
>
> 1 Samuel 16:7

Parents need to follow the example of the Lord and look at their teenager's heart and not the outward appearance. On the other hand, they should not ignore the fact that the world *does* judge people by their outward appearance. Society always will believe a person's behavior, intelligence, attitudes, or lifestyle can be determined by his outward looks.

An Example of Love and Tolerance

Suppose some guy with long hair, one earring, a scraggly beard, and ragged clothes comes into church. Most people there would automatically assume he is a "hippie" or a bum who is not saved and who probably is into drugs. Right? Even many Christians look upon the outward appearance of man, instead of being careful to reserve judgment.

Christians should be setting an example of love and tolerance to the rest of the world. That is an important lesson for teenagers to learn as well. How will sinners know that Christian teens have something they need if those teenagers act and treat them as everyone else does? If Christian teens condemn and categorize people for the way they look, then what makes them different from unregenerate teenagers? Nothing!

Teenagers should be told that they are an example for the lost. How are the lost to know that Christians have something life-changing and something they need, or that Christians are different in any way, if they all look the same? That point sets a balance or a guideline for establishing standards for how teenagers look and dress.

First Thessalonians 5:22 says, **Abstain from all appearance of evil**, and that has two purposes. The first is for the Christian's own good. If he will avoid things he does not believe are truly sinful but look questionable, then there is no risk of becoming involved with something evil because he misjudged it.

Christians do not always know the total truth about everything in the world; and it would be terrible to become tangled up in something sinful after ignoring the subtle warning signals around it.

The second reason to avoid any appearance of evil is to prevent others who might follow in your footsteps from making wrong decisions as a result of your example. You do not want anyone to stumble or be offended by the things you do. Mature Christians continually are being watched by unbelievers, carnal Christians, and young Christians. Some of them are looking for an excuse to convince themselves you are not "real." People with negative outlooks do not like it when you talk about prosperity and health or when you are happy on Monday mornings.

When I was a teenager, I had some friends who had the same attitudes and values I did. They were bitter, rebellious people involved with drugs and full of hatred. However, their parents were very strict and controlled them enough to make it look as if they were "square." These friends would go to church, and they looked like "sweet little Christians." But they were full of sin. We do need to look as neat and nice as possible, but we need to be careful not to judge others by such appearances.

Regarding clothes and fashions, parents should consider how much freedom to allow their teenager. If he is rebellious and difficult to deal with, then parents should be a little stricter with him. When a teenager is bold enough to throw his weight around a little with mom and dad, I guarantee that he acts five times worse at school and with his friends. Most teens will usually be more cautious with their parents. Then they let loose their more extreme behavior away from home.

One thing to be aware of is that a teenager sometimes will use clothes and personal grooming as protective barriers to mask how he feels about himself. If he feels inferior or unworthy, he may strive to look as sharp as possible in order to gain approval and admiration. If he feels unloved or unnoticed, he might go for a bizarre look to get attention from other people.

Fashions Change With the Times

Timing is a key factor when you look at things such as clothes, hairstyles, jewelry, and makeup. A look at history will show that for a Christian woman to wear red lipstick, pants, or even a red dress to church in the 1940s or 1950s would have been highly unacceptable.

A Spirit-filled woman I know from a denominational church wanted for years to get her ears pierced but she did not get up enough courage to go against the traditions of her church until recently when she was past fifty years of age. She had always been taught it was sinful for a woman to pierce her ears. This may seem funny now, but a few years ago, it was serious business.

The church's attitude about men getting their ears pierced today is the same as it was about women a few years ago. For a long time, only homosexual men wore earrings, but now that is changing. A few years from now, who knows?

A woman wearing makeup in some churches a few decades ago would automatically have been considered promiscuous. To relate this to today: Teenagers who are always on the leading edge of fashion are regarded as "bad" or rebellious. They are the ones wearing the latest wild or radical fashions, or the ones who have the latest hairstyle, and the more weird it is, the better.

After seeing the new styles for a while, people cease to be appalled and begin to take them for granted. Soon Christian teenagers are wearing the same fashions as their peers in the world, and people no longer consider that fashion a sign of being worldly or rebellious.

A good example is parachute pants. When they first came out, only the rebellious teenagers wore them. The more zippers were on the pants and the baggier they were, the more radical they were. Very rebellious teens looked for the flashiest ones they could find. But after a year or so, parachute pants became accepted and were toned down into conservative tastes. Made of silk, they usually only had a couple of zippers and a pocket on the side. No big deal anymore. Quite a difference from their first appearance. Now they are outdated, old-fashioned and found only at thrift stores. However in years to come, they will probably be back.

Now they no longer command the attention or gain the reaction they got in the beginning when only rock stars or movies stars were wearing them. Fashion designers tend to be the nonconformist elements in society — and many of them *are* homosexual. However, as I have shown, even fashions that seem very extreme at first sight eventually become acceptable and may even end up being fairly tame.

This generalization cannot be applied across the board, however. I do not believe having a blue-dyed Mohawk hairstyle ever will be acceptable or in good taste for a Christian! Except maybe for evangelistic purposes by some rock bands.

Maintain a Balance

At our church school, we like to maintain a balanced attitude in regard to styles. Students are trained to feel good about themselves in general, which then expresses itself through their grooming and personal appearance. Teenagers like to dress nicely for school.

Young men in our school are not made to feel like freaks when they wear ties and blazers. Their friends and classmates do not look at them as if they were old-fashioned, religious, or "antique" in their tastes. On the other hand, our teenagers feel just as comfortable in casual clothes that are clean, neat, and up-to-date in style.

We simply encourage all of them to be happy and relaxed about their appearances and not get all caught up with trying to impress everyone else. Training them early in life to maintain a balanced attitude is the key to their accepting themselves and being accepted, where clothes, hairstyles, and makeup are concerned.

6
Media

Media can be a tremendous teaching tool when used appropriately. We have been able to point out to our youth group many false notions young people pick up in their lives by discussing situations portrayed in movies and television. If parents will watch the same movies and television programs as their children, they can intercept lies about life (which teenagers eventually will hear, no matter how strict parents are), and be able to point out the truth.

There are extremes in parental regulation of media just as in other areas. Some parents would not own a television set and believe movie theaters are the equivalent of a house of prostitution. Then there are others who are not concerned about what goes into their children's minds, because they feel their teaching and the foundation received at home will overcome any negative input. I feel the best approach is somewhere in the center of these two.

There are excellent movies and good television programs in the world today. However, there is no question that the evil presented in television and movies will influence the minds of anyone who watches them. Regulation of what goes into our minds and into our children's minds is mandatory to build good treasures in the heart.

It is up to the parents to differentiate between the good films and programs that are educational and/or entertaining and those that promote sin.

Our Personal Standards

The standards my wife and I set in our own home were established and communicated quite some time ago. R-rated movies are out of the question. PG-13 movies can only be seen by our daughter after my wife or I have previewed them. Most of the time, it is the same for a PG movie, unless it is highly recommended or endorsed by someone I know and trust. In regard to judging movies, there are not many people we trust — only those who have teenagers, or who lead teenagers, and who have great integrity.

Some people consider our standard too loose, and others think we are too rigid. However, where our daughter is concerned, we feel the above guidelines are safe and effective. It is the same one my wife and I personally live by. If others feel their teenager needs stricter standards, then that must be their decision.

Regarding television, regulation of the quantity watched as well as the quality is mandatory for a spiritually healthy Christian teenager. Studies show that by the age of eighteen, young people will have spent more time in front of the television set than anywhere else, including school. Another study estimates that by graduation, the average high school student has spent twenty-two thousand hours watching television, nearly twice the amount of time spent in twelve years of school.[1]

Obviously, we must limit the amount of movie-watching and television-watching our teenagers do, as well as what they are watching. Parents need to be aware of how much sex and how much fantasy is being portrayed on many programs.

Teenagers are particularly prone to realistic-looking Cinderella stories where Prince Charming rescues the

---

[1] McDowell, Josh. *Why Wait? What You Need To Know About the Teen Sexuality Crisis* (Here's Life Publishing, 1987).

troubled Cinderella from her life of drudgery as they fall in love at first sight and live happily ever after. Even some Christian fiction writers are guilty of this kind of unrealistic portrayal of love and marriage.

Relationship after relationship has been established on this type of romantic fantasy and is a major reason why more than half of the marriages in America end in divorce. "Cinderella" finds out "Prince Charming" has a bad attitude, and he finds out there was a good reason why she was in the drudgery in which he found her!

Movies, Films Usually Are Fantasies

Television and movie producers know teenagers thrive on identifying emotionally with the characters in these stories. So they portray their wildest dreams as if they really could come to pass, but it is all Hollywood, not reality. However, teenagers do not make this discernment without someone to point out the reality of the situation.

When our daughter was very young, we began pointing out, generally in a ridiculing manner, the discrepancy between such fantasy and reality. Early on, *she* became able to point out such discrepancies. We mentioned things such as that television never shows the people who "party" and drink too much, in the bathroom later throwing up and doctoring their headaches, or visiting the doctor to take care of their venereal disease, or the anguish felt by people caught in the middle of their sin.

The communications media is such a powerful and prevalent influence in our society that it cannot be overlooked. We do not need to fear what might happen to our teens from watching television, but we do need to be aware of the dangers and monitor it. If their foundation in Christ is solid and the input they get from media is regulated, they will rise above any such influence.

Ye are of God, little children, and have overcome them:
because *greater is he that is in you, than he that is in the world.*
1 John 4:4

7

Grades

Grades and schoolwork are the number one responsibility for teenagers outside of their commitment to the Lord and to their families. Schoolwork is their equivalent of an adult's job. If they are failing in their schoolwork, they are failing in one of their top priorities.

True success is not measured by wearing the right clothes, listening to the right music, or watching the right movies. An adult who cannot hold on to a job, or is chronically late to work, is both immature and a failure at handling responsibilities.

It is no different for young people. They must learn the importance of being responsible at an early age. Parents must help their children to develop a good attitude about school in preparation for the time they will have a job and be on their own.

Teens need to have a desire to excel and be successful, while they are still students so that those positive attitudes will carry over to their adult lives.

However, the teen's natural aptitudes and abilities must be taken into consideration when setting standards. Some are more talented in art, music, and literary subjects than in math or science. With others, it is vice versa.

Teens should be taught to work diligently even in subjects that are difficult for them, because the knowledge will be beneficial. But lower grade levels are acceptable in those courses than in those subjects they love and are good at.

Every mentally and emotionally sound Christian teenager should earn grades no lower than "B's"; and, their goal should be to achieve straight "A's." Also, they should be well-liked, as well as good students, athletes, and musicians — if that is where their talents lie.

The reason Christian teens should be exceptional is that the Holy Spirit will work in them to bring all things to their remembrance, if they will allow Him to and believe that He will. Because of having supernatural abilities from God, they have an advantage over non-saved students when it comes to studying and taking exams.

Past Training Has an Effect

Before parents can expect their teenagers to become top students, they need to consider what their training has been up to this point. If teenagers have had no teaching on how to do schoolwork or how to be disciplined in school, a sudden demand to get straight "A's" would be not only unfair but unrealistic.

It is unwise of parents to expect teens to turn a situation around in a few months that has taken years to develop. It will take some time to retrain them in ways of good discipline and study.

In high school, I was able to earn "B's" and a few "A's" without a lot of trouble — thanks to my parents' demands. But I really did not know how to study. It was a different story in college. Good grades were not easy any longer, and I needed straight "A's" to get accepted into medical school.

After the first quarter when I did not do so well, I realized that my roommate had a method that allowed him to succeed in his classes. So I watched him and learned how to study. From then on, I got almost straight "A's" and graduated with a very high gradepoint average — all because someone trained me how to study, not because I am a natural-born genius!

It is the parents' responsibility to train their children how to study. If they do not know how themselves, they can get advice from teachers, or friends who do know how. Parents also should teach their teens to be disciplined by making sure he completes his schoolwork. Perhaps, a teenager can be encouraged to study with other good students who will help him to develop and achieve more.

When the young person who used to "just get by" sees "A's" and "B's" on his report cards for the first time, his self-worth will shoot up. Also, good grades will be vital when a teenager grows up and moves out into the work force. He will be competing with everyone else his age for the prime jobs. The attitudes, discipline, and self-image people develop in their teenage years have a powerful influence on their adult lives.

Another really important reason for parents encouraging, inspiring, and demanding their children perform well is because of the erroneous mental picture their children will create of themselves if they do poorly.

Young people left to their own decisions without the proper training, will generally do only what they feel like doing or what they are interested in.

What happens in cases where this is allowed to happen is that a student performs poorly in a particular subject then judges his ability and intelligence concerning that subject based upon his performance.

The truth of the matter is their performance was based upon their lack of desire and lack of discipline not their lack of brains. Unfortunately they do not have the ability to discern this fact. Consequently we have many people walking around convinced they are not very smart and performing far below their potential.

The really sad thing about this is that when they grow older and their desires change, they exclude themselves from being able to do something they would really like to do. This is because they have convinced themselves, by their past performance, that they are incapable of doing it.

Parents must help their children learn how truly intelligent and capable they are by encouraging, admonishing and demanding that they perform well in school.

Therefore, the training ground for a successful life begins with schoolwork.

All the other responsibilities and levels of independence a teenager wants should be determined by how well he is handling his number-one responsibility: schoolwork. If he is getting "D's" and "F's" and struggling just to pass into the next grade — *and he could do better* — his parents should not be giving him too many privileges and independence.

Sports Are No Substitute for Education

Athletics is an example of a privilege that should be restricted if schoolwork is not up to par. Sports are good for young people, but they are no substitute for a good education. Even non-Christian parents realize their children should not invest time and energy into competitive sports unless an acceptable gradepoint average is being maintained.

Christian parents should have even higher standards for their teen:

- How much free time will he have?
- How often can he date?
- How late can he, or she, stay out on Friday nights?
- How many weekends may he spend with friends?
- How many hobbies can he have?

These are examples of things that should be determined by how well schoolwork is being done.

8

Friends

Friends are vitally important to teenagers, and parents have the right and the obligation to regulate who those friends are, although teenagers usually do not like this. However, parents are responsible for teenagers' training as long as those young people live at home, and that training includes what they learn from their friends.

Make no friendship with an angry man; and with a furious man thou shalt not go:

Lest thou learn his ways, and get a snare to thy soul.
Proverbs 22:24,25

This is just one of the wisdom principles of the Word concerning choosing one's companions and friends. A teenager who hangs around other teens who are hostile, angry, and rebellious will end up learning their ways and messing up his own life.

This advice also applies to other negative behaviors, whether it is a lustful spirit, a criminal spirit, or a worldly spirit. A teenager will end up doing what he learns from his friends, so his parents not only have the right but the obligation to regulate who those friends are.

My wife, daughter, and I once lived in a neighborhood with children whose background was very negative. These were the only children nearby of Christina's age, but we had to refuse to let her play with them. There was no way we wanted her to learn their habits, attitudes, and behavior.

It was tough to take this position with our daughter, but we had to make her aware of the dangers involved. Also, we were obligated to protect the security of her mind and spirit as well as the safety of her body.

There has to be something happening: Young people who develop relationships with negative people will begin to exhibit the same negative habits and behavior.

If parents see their teenager constantly drawn to the wrong crowd, this is an indication something needs to change in the home and with their own teen, not just with the friends. There needs to be more communication, self-examination, love and perhaps some counsel from others.

However, even the best of teenagers need to have their friendships examined and monitored by the parents.

Do Not Walk With the Ungodly

This is another reason why parents must not allow their teenagers, or even younger children, to "get in with the wrong crowd."

> **Blessed is the man that walketh not in the counsel of the ungodly, nor standeth in the way of sinners, nor sitteth in the seat of the scornful.**
>
> **But his delight is in the law of the Lord; and in his law doth he meditate day and night.**
>
> **Psalm 1:1,2**

The ungodly have plenty of advice to give!

They will tell a teenager things like, "Ah, that church stuff doesn't matter! What is the big deal about listening to a little rock music or going to a movie once in a while? They do not even want you to go to a dance? Will you go to hell or something just because you went to a dance?"

Sinners always will do their own thing, so Christians had better stop walking according to the way of the sinner if they want to be blessed.

Scornful people are mockers, those who like to "put down" or ridicule godly things and godly people. They are motivated by pride or lack of self-worth. They feel that putting down other people makes them superior. It builds up their ego. If parents want their teenager to be blessed and enjoy life, they must eliminate their relationships with scornful friends, with those who mock the Christian lifestyle.

Avoiding close friendships does not mean absolutely no contact, however. Some parents try to keep their teenager away from everyone, perhaps even to the extent of teaching them at home rather than sending them to public school. There is nothing wrong with home schooling as long as that child is getting out and socializing with other godly teenagers.

Parents must realize that they need to oversee their teenager's friends and lifestyle, but they also need to realize they cannot completely isolate him from the rest of the world.

Jesus prayed to the Father concerning his disciples:

I pray not that thou shouldest take them out of the world, but that thou shouldest keep them from the evil

John 17:15

Instead of trying to isolate the teenager, parents should simply monitor those whom he associates with regularly.

Make the Bible the Basis of Reasoning

Parents need to use the Word of God in their reasoning. If a friend of their child does not measure up to the Word, parents should talk to the teen very bluntly and clearly about what the Word says. This is what I mean by "monitoring" friends.

Parents could tell their son or daughter, "I know you like this person, but the truth is that he is ungodly, scornful, worldly, and actually sinful. According to the Word, I am responsible for you, and I must insist that you not be involved with that person any longer."

Then parents must make every effort to help their teenager fill the void of that severed relationship with other friendships with godly teenagers. Parents may have to chauffeur their teen around a lot to get him to the right activities or, possibly, even move out of one neighborhood into another to meet that need.

The Bible has other advice on what kind of friendships to develop and on how to deal with problems between friends. One such verse is Proverbs 28:23, which deals with the results of telling the truth as opposed to insincerity.

He that rebuketh a man afterwards shall find more favour than he that flattereth with the tongue.

Suppose you are angry with someone for what he did or said, but you say to others, "I know he really did not mean that. He was just 'in the flesh' right then. I am going to pray for him, give this situation to the Lord, and forgive that person."

That is wonderful — if it is the truth. Often, however, the person is still mad and only paying lip service to forgiveness, or outwardly conforming to righteousness. Inwardly, many times the offended person is still seething, which makes his remarks insincere.

Instead of confronting the person about the offense so that it can be resolved and forgiven — and instead of admitting that anger also needs to be repented of and forgiveness received — the offended person is acting as if there is no problem. Usually, however, he will continue to stew about the offense. Then the next time he sees the one who offended him, he may act friendly. That brings him into the sin of hypocrisy. He is still upset but pretending not to be.

What Is Flattery?

"Flattering with the tongue" means bragging on that person or paying someone a compliment when you know he needs to be rebuked or confronted. Christians should understand that "walking in love" does not mean always being nice and polite. Sometimes it means having the courage to rebuke others, for their benefit, who do hurtful or harmful things.

I am not talking about judging others or "straightening out" another Christian. I am talking about personal incidents between you and another person. I am talking about leaving your gift at the altar and going and making peace with your brother. (Matt. 5:24.)

For instance, such an incident in a teenager's life might be a girl who is "stood up" by a young man who has made a date with her. Instead of ignoring what happened or acting as if it was no big deal, she should "rebuke" that young man — not accuse him or scold him in anger.

Here is an example of such a comment:

"You know what? I did not like it one bit when you didn't show up for our date. You didn't call, or try to get in touch with me at all. That was both wrong and irresponsible. I think you should understand that when you make a commitment and give your word to do something, you should make every effort to be there or let the other person know in advance why you cannot."

The person on the receiving end of this will not feel good at the moment. But if this rebuke is delivered in a kind and caring manner, he may realize that the girl is trying to help him mature. This rebuke was delivered in order to promote growth and change, not to vent a bad attitude and hatred.

Making excuses for another's wrongdoing or irresponsibility amounts to flattery. A comment that excuses or condones really is "hating" that person, because you are hurting not helping him.

Saying, "Hey, it's a busy life. It happens to me too sometimes," will not help him to change. Also, he may think the girl is not upset, which is not the truth. The person who will confront and rebuke is a better friend than someone who just lets the person continue on being involved in sin. Parents need to help their teenager find friends who will be honest with him, as well as help him learn to be honest with his friends.

Rebuking Should Be Done in Love

Rebuking, or confronting someone else, should always be done in an attitude of love and peace. If you can honestly forgive someone and feel a rebuke would not benefit that person, that is fine. Praise the Lord! However, if you find you are still angry even after you have "turned it over to the Lord" and spoken forgiveness, then you have not truly forgiven. It may take talking to the person about the incident to clear it up for both your sakes.

Otherwise, a wall will continue to separate the two of you, and it will not go away with time. Perhaps that wall is not as visible as time goes by, but it is still there blocking a true flow of the love of God between the two of you.

Junior high students seem to be the age group that finds comfort in banding together and putting down others who are not part of their group. This age group likes to form little cliques, gossip, and pick on their peers. Negative, hurtful behavior like this can kill a youth group by spreading embarrassment, loneliness, and fear.

A young person subjected to this kind of treatment suffers just as much as an adult who is going through a separation or divorce. It is a horrible feeling to know that other teens are gossiping about you, or are mad at you and do not want anything to do with you!

Parents should be sensitive to their children's feelings and remember how they felt at that age. The world of the teenager can be brutal, particularly for those who are not exactly in step with the others. It is important for parents to help their teens find the kinds of friends who will be honest and forthright in love.

Teens need friends who will openly tell them when they are acting weird, dressing funny, or just generally messing up. It is much better for a teen to be confronted or rebuked in private from a friend who is trying to help than to get "hit between the eyes" with criticism from a hostile crowd.

Those kinds of friends will help a teenager to become a strong and mighty man or woman of valor. Many parents like to think of themselves as their teenager's counselor and advisor, but his peer group has a lot of input into what he achieves and how stable he will be emotionally, spiritually, and physically.

If parents want their teen to have young counselors (friends) who are honest and open, then they should set the example by cultivating the same kind of adult friends, those who will provide the same challenges to their own growth.

> **Without counsel purposes are disappointed: but in the multitude of counsellors they are established.**
> **Proverbs 15:22**

> **For by wise counsel thou shalt make thy war: and in multitude of counsellors there is safety.**
> **Proverbs 24:6**

Some Friends Can Be 'Poison'

There are times when parents may just have to be blunt and say, "No, you cannot be around that person any longer. They cannot come over, and you cannot go over to their house. You cannot call them on the phone. This is the end of your relationship."

If parents do not intervene, there is a real danger that teenager may be "poisoned" by the negative attitudes and actions of his ill-chosen friends. Proverbs 13:20 says:

> **He that walketh with wise men shall be wise: but a companion of fools shall be destroyed.**

You do not have to be a fool to be destroyed, just a companion of them. Parents cannot allow their children to be destroyed because of their friends. Proverbs 27:17 says:

> **As iron sharpeneth iron; so a man sharpeneth the countenance of his friend.**

Friends will influence how "sharp," good, and right someone becomes. If the friends are negative (rebellious or worldly, or depressed) or they are not interested in going all out for God, their influence will impact your teenager in the same way. Friends who are "religious," as opposed to truly living for Christ, also can be a negative influence in a teenager's life because they are living a life of legalism and hypocrisy.

Either way, parents have the right and responsibility to help regulate the kinds of friends their teenagers make.

9

Church Attendance

Parents are responsible for the spiritual training of their young people as well as all of the natural things that we have been talking about.

Some people have the funny notion that letting their children grow up without any church experience will prepare them to make an open-minded, honest decision about what kind of religion they want to choose when they are adults.

That is absolute "hogwash!" Proverbs 22:6 says:

> Train up a child in the way he should go: and when he is old, he will not depart from it.

Deuteronomy 6:6-9 says:

> And these words, which I command thee this day, shall be in thine heart:
>
> And thou shalt teach them diligently unto thy children, and shalt talk of them when thou sittest in thine house, and when thou walkest by the way, and when thou liest down, and when thou risest up.
>
> And thou shalt bind them for a sign upon thine hand, and they shall be as frontlets between thine eyes.
>
> And thou shalt write them upon the posts of thy house, and on thy gates.

Those may be Old Testament verses, but the principle is for believers of all ages: Have the words of the Lord in your heart and remind yourself and your children of them continuously. That is how you get wisdom from the Lord.

If parents want their teenagers to have an equal balance between positive and negative input, they would have to be in church fifty to sixty hours a week!

67

The devil and his demonic kingdom is continually bombarding their minds with an evil way of life. The deck is stacked in the devil's favor because the world is under his rule and influence.

Most Christian parents realize that it is critical for their children to be involved in church and to receive spiritual training. Their only questions usually involve just how much training, what type of training, and how old a teenager should be when he is allowed to make his own decisions about when and how often he wants to attend church.

Church Involvement Is Critical

I have met with families quite often to talk about who should be in charge of these decisions. A lot of teenagers come into these discussions with the mistaken idea that they are going to straighten out their parents' thinking.

They rationalize, "Hey, I'm seventeen years old, and it's time I decide what I am going to do with my life. You can't make me change, anyway. I don't have to accept what is going on in that church. I don't have to do what they say. You can't make me believe it."

They are correct when they say no one can make them believe. Nevertheless, it is the parents' responsibility to train them up in the way they should go, which includes at least hearing the Word of God, even if they sit in church mad.

If parents have a teenager who resists them on this particular issue, they should just say, "Okay, the Bible says I am supposed to train you up in the way you should go. Now what part of your life does that cover:

Does it mean making sure you have clothes to wear?

Does it mean providing you with a warm and safe home where you can live and sleep?

Does it include providing you with food to eat?

If it covers all of these physical things, why should it not cover the spiritual or mental things?"

What can a teen say to refute this reasoning? Nothing.

If a young person is ready to be responsible for his own spiritual training, then he is ready to be responsible for his own physical needs as well. He can handle paying for his own food, transportation, rent, clothing, and whatever else he needs. If he is ready for the one, he is ready for the other.

If he wants mom and dad to take care of him, then they have the right to take care of every area of his life. That is only fair. He may not like it, but there is nothing he can say about it.

Most parents will not run into this problem, unless they have an extremely rebellious teenager. Other parents, who have just been saved or just become seriously involved with the Word, may see some negative reactions from their teens initially. However, the children should settle down when there has been a little time to adjust to the changes taking place in the parents.

Use Judgment and Discretion

On the other hand, parents should not try to make their children become involved with every church activity that is available. For example, a teen should not have to join the youth group if he does not want to. Parents should just let him know the group is there and let him see they are having fun as Christians. He needs to see that this group is not made up of "nerds."

It will be a real eye-opener for a reluctant teen to see that Christian young people can be up-to-date, look good, and be full of fun. Even if he refuses to build relationships with Christian teens, still he needs to hear the Word on a regular basis. Summer camps and other such outings are a good place to begin.

So be *flexible* to this degree: Let it be his choice whether to participate in the youth service or attend adult services with mom and dad. But be *inflexible* on the rule that he *will* attend one of the services as long as he lives at home.

This is another place where parents need to be consistent and be the example. If parents say church attendance is not optional, than there must be a regular weekly commitment to church by the whole family. If there is not, the teenager will immediately see the hypocrisy and lessen his respect for the parents' authority. Of course, they may say nothing about it because they may like getting out of going to church as much as possible but their attitude towards mom and dad will be poor.

Another thing to examine is the church itself. If the child or teenager is complaining about the church and you are not deeply committed to the church, examine the possibility of finding a church more acceptable to the whole family. If you are committed to the church and feel you should not leave, do not stop there. Perhaps the youth group needs help or is inadequate and you should investigate. You may find out there is good reason why your child does not want to participate. Perhaps you can help the youth group in some way or if that doesn't work, you may look for other Christian youth activities or other youth groups to supplement what is available at your church.

Concerning discipline and church, it is not good to use positive church outings for discipline. In other words, if a teen needs disciplining through restriction on his activities, it would be better to make it hobbies or school activities rather than church functions. The exception would be if the church outing was simply a "fun" event without any spiritual content.

10
Curfews

A curfew is the time determined by the parents for the teenager to be home from any activities.

This time limit should be based on the teenager's age and on the need for a certain amount of sleep each night. Moral implications and safety also should be taken into consideration.

Parents should make every effort to allow a teenager as much time when attending an event as is reasonably possible. They certainly do not want their child to get the idea they do not want him to have any fun!

If there is a special event chaperoned by responsible adults, then teens should be allowed extensions of their curfews. If the leader of the event is a responsible, Christian adult, parents should be able to trust that person to handle the situation.

Of course, parents should be careful to check out the "responsible adults" who are chaperoning teenage activities. There are many adults, even church members, who are irresponsible and extremely permissive. Parents should find out the beliefs of those in charge of events, what type of behavior they will allow, and how much control they will have over the event.

If a teenager is going to an event chaperoned by enough responsible adults for the number of young people attending, then the parents should let them go, have fun, and stay for a long time.

Slumber parties with an adult to monitor the conversation and behavior of teenagers are good activities to allow. This assumes you know the chaperones well enough to trust them. It will not hurt teenagers, once in a while on a weekend night, to stay up until 3 or 4 a.m. This should not be a regular happening, of course, but it could be a special treat.

To a teenager, staying up all night is something memorable and exciting. When they are in a safe situation, parents should let them go and have a good time.

Also, teenagers should be allowed to go to church youth group activities if they desire. When a teenager does attend a late-night party or outing, his parents should not expect him to do all his regular chores the next day. He will need a break to catch up on his sleep.

When parents set curfews, they should define what kinds of places their teenagers may go and what kinds of activities will be allowed. This is only using common sense.

Factors involved in determining the actual time for a teen to be home such as:

- Age
- Previous record of responsibilities and times of independence
- The location of the activity
- The chaperons
- The other teens who will be participating.
  a) maturity
  b) male or female

11

Chores

The subject of household responsibilities, or chores, has caused both shock and excitement for me in dealing with teens in my youth group. One of the special courses I teach is a series of ten basic leadership skills for young people. One topic concerns being led of the Spirit, and the bottom line of this teaching is "living a disciplined life."

Associate youth pastor Steve Murray and I both talked to the young people during one session of this series about cleaning their rooms and keeping things in order.

One morning, Steve asked, "How many of you have started to keep your rooms clean and neat since we have talked about being led of the Spirit?"

About two-thirds of the class raised their hands!

My first reaction was, "Great!"

But my second reaction was to wonder why their parents were not already on top of that situation. Those teenagers already should have been taking care of their rooms!

Teens will not feel good about home or have a strong sense of self-worth if their rooms are not neat, clean, and in order. Everyone feels better when their home is clean and organized. What your living space looks like is a reflection of what is going on in your mind.

Having junk, or even good things, piled all over the room is not going to make someone feel good. If your surroundings are messy, so probably is your mind and your life.

Allowing teenagers to live this way means you are allowing them to develop lifelong bad habits. Probably, the disorganization and mess will only grow worse as they get older. More than likely, as adults, their homes will be disaster areas — if they do not learn to be organized and neat now.

Do You Have a Sloth Living With You?

Parents should look into their teenager's bedroom and see if they have a "sloth" living with them!

> I went by the field of the slothful, and by the vineyard of the man void of understanding;
>
> And lo, it was all grown over with thorns, and nettles had covered the face thereof, and the stone wall thereof was broken down.
>
> Then I saw, and considered it well: I looked upon it, and received instruction.
>
> Yet a little sleep, a little slumber, a little folding of the hands to sleep:
>
> So shall thy poverty come as one that travelleth; and thy want as an armed man.
>
> **Proverbs 24:30-34.**

What a dose of instruction and wisdom! Unless a teenager learns to overcome any tendencies to slothfulness and clean up his messy room, he will be involved with poverty and be unsatisfied all of his life. He will get "ripped off," figuratively speaking.

Unless his parents train him to be diligent and take care of what he has, his life will be as if an armed man sneaked up and demanded, "Give me everything you've got!"

Teenagers and parents have a joint responsibility to make sure they diligently maintain the things under their direct control, such as their school lockers, their bedrooms, their bicycles, and their pets. However, living as part of a family also means they should have other household chores in areas that affect everyone else in the family. These are responsibilities for which they should not get rewards.

Why should they receive a wage for doing work in their own home, the place where they live and which they help to mess up?

So, next, let's discuss what teenagers *should* get paid for.

12

Allowances

Allowances are not only good, but necessary, if parents want their children to learn how to handle finances, create a budget, and tithe.

But teens should not be paid to clean up their own messes, or to help clean their own homes.

If parents want to give teens extra money, then allow them to earn it through additional responsibilities outside of housecleaning. These could be things such as straightening the garage, washing the family car, or painting the fence.

Lamentations 3:27 says:

It is good for a man that he bear the yoke in his youth.

In other words, he should have responsibilities while he is young. Parents should be training that young person to handle responsibility with a good attitude, for he will have responsibilities the rest of his life.

If parents allow a teen to walk around with a lousy attitude because he has to clean the toilet, he always will hate doing it. He not only will hate household chores, but he will more than likely end up hating his job because he will not know how to handle menial tasks cheerfully.

Parents have to tell their teenager, "These are your responsibilities, and I don't want to hear any griping. This is real life, and the Bible says to rejoice in the Lord always. What is so bad about cleaning house anyway?"

Of course, *some* parents may have to change their own attitudes about housework or menial outside chores, because it will be a lot easier if their children see them making the same efforts they are demanding. It will be a lot easier if the parents enjoy a neat and orderly house. A teenager needs to realize that the results of hard work will be rewarding and worthwhile.

Back to allowances, parents should teach their children how to handle finances from the time they are very young. Even if they only get a dollar a week, it is good training in managing money. They need to learn about tithing, giving offerings, saving money, and living off what is left.

Most children who are not trained will immediately spend all their money without thought for the future, because foolishness is bound in the heart of a child. (Prov. 22:15.)

Financial Principles

Even young children should begin to learn good financial principles. One principle is that people should live on 70 percent of their income, save ten percent and give away 20 percent (tithes, offerings, charitable contributions). Parents who live by this principle should train their children to use the same principle.

By the time they are adults, they will not get themselves in debt over their heads. Instead of charging things and running up credit card bills, they will be so conditioned to live by this principle that they will just naturally prosper. They will be fiscally responsible, because they are giving and saving as they manage to live within the limits of the remainder. Parents would be doing their children a wonderful service if they made them live up to this.

I attended a secular seminar for businessmen, in which the teacher told of driving his child into the ghetto of his city and explaining how people who do not apply the principles of the Bible to their lives will end up living in that kind of poverty.

Many poverty-stricken people have simply "learned" that type of lifestyle and regard it as inevitable. However, it can happen to anyone foolish enough to ignore the truths about finances and responsibile living that are found in the Bible.

13

Dating

The area of dating has the greatest amount of potential for disaster of any other area of life for teenagers. For this reason, dating should be carefully and prayerfully considered by parents. It can be an exciting and enjoyable time for the teen as well as the parents, if certain guidelines and understandings are established.

There are extremes on both sides of the question, as is usual. There are parents who allow their children to become involved in dating early and operate on blind trust that everything is going to be all right.

Also, I have seen many a parent attempting to live out his, or her, own dating fantasy through the teenager, all at the expense of the teen, of course.

Then there are those who will not let a child date until the right marriage partner is found, and of course, the "right" partner is the one chosen by the parent!

Both of these extremes are detrimental to a teenager and often to the parent-child relationship, as well. A dating relationship should be a natural progression of growth in each person's life, not an all-consuming interest that overshadows all other aspects of life.

The world teaches that "true love" only comes through relationships that are portrayed as involving pre-marital or extra-marital sex. Movies and television programs present wonderful-looking, but sinful, romantic relationships. Those portrayals literally are fantasies and not true-to-life at all.

The important thing for parents to understand (or perhaps simply to remember) is the impact of this stage on a teenager. If parents take this stage as seriously as it warrants, they will not deal with dating and sexual relationships lightly or leave it up to the teenager to form his own opinions. Parents need to help mold and form godly and sober attitudes about dating in their children. This area of life is nothing to play around with.

Being Overcome by the Flesh

Even church-going teenagers, who are led by the Holy Spirit and are involved with things of God, can be overcome by the flesh and fall into fornication. The same warning applies to the best church members, the best prayer warriors, or the best Bible students. Every Christian still has a body subject to all types of carnal desires.

In the early Eighties, statistics showed that, by age twenty, 81 percent of today's unmarried males and 67 percent of today's unmarried females have had sexual intercourse.[1] They also show that Christian teenagers have nearly the same statistics as unsaved young people.

One example is a teenage relationships survey, which revealed that "religion-conscious girls are 86 percent more likely to say it is important to be a virgin at marriage than nonreligion-conscious girls. However, religion-conscious girls are only 14 percent more likely to be virgins than nonreligion-conscious girls."[2]

I am sure these statistics have not changed for the better in ten years. What they reveal is that *knowledge is not enough*. Discipline and responsibility also must be involved. Christian

---

[1]*Teenage Pregnancy: The Problem That Hasn't Gone Away* (New York: Guttmacher Institute, 1981).

[2]Nonkin, Leslie Jane. *I Wish My Parents Understood* (New York: Penguin Books: 1982).

girls get pregnant. Christians get venereal diseases. Christian girls have abortions. Christian young people definitely do have sexual intercourse!

Often, such relationships are not planned ahead of time or deliberate, because most Christian teens will not willfully plan to disobey the Word of God. However, in the heat of certain moments while dating, their will is far more influenced by emotional and sexual feelings than by spiritual beliefs. Many times, they give in to the body and the emotions.

Even if there is not actual sin involved, Christian teens should be taught to shun the very appearance of evil. (1 Thess. 5:22.) When a girl and boy are together alone often, many people automatically assume they are sexually involved. Teenagers particularly make this assumption, because they frequently talk about sex and intimate relationships. This area of their lives is new and almost overpowering at times.

Parents should talk to their teens about reasons for dating and help them determine if they are only interested in having fun or if they are seriously looking for a marriage partner. If they just want to enjoy companionship and have fun with members of the opposite sex, they should be told to make these encounters safe from temptation by participating in activities that have other teens involved — crowd events.

Teens and their parents should discuss what love really is, because you would be surprised what misconceptions teens sometimes have about parental concerns.

Many teens have this attitude: "Well, what is the matter with being in love anyway? We're not going to bed with each other. Adults think if we go out with someone, we are going to get pregnant or contract a social disease."

Sure, parents are concerned about those things, but primarily and usually, they are concerned that teens will suffer emotional hurts and be distracted from seeking after God. Many young people can become so consumed with their dating relationships that their lives almost become controlled by them.

A Christian's life should be a testimony of love to the world.

What *Is* True Love?

I tell teenagers this:

"You should know what you are getting involved in. Ask yourself what you are doing with your life concerning dating. What are you doing to the other person's life? When you become involved with those intimate, romantic feelings, you are not just affecting your own life. You also are affecting people all around you as well as the individual with whom you are involved."

Jesus told us true love is serving other people. The epitome of true love was the Father sending Jesus to die on the cross. Jesus sacrificing His life for the benefit of mankind is true love.

> **A new commandment I give unto you, That ye love one another; as I have loved you, that ye also love one another.**
>
> **By this shall all men know that ye are my disciples, if ye have love one to another.**
>
> **John 13:34,35**

When Jesus said this, He had just finished washing the feet of the disciples and demonstrating real love in action.

Love is not just some emotion. However, the feelings surrounding fleshly love can be very powerful. As children move into their teenage years and their bodies begin to change, they often will experience strong feelings of attraction for the opposite sex.

A guy may be walking down the hall at school when he sees this cute girl. Their eyes meet, she smiles at him, and suddenly his heart jumps into his throat, and his hands get all sweaty. A strong desire comes over him to find out her name and where her locker is located.

Then, through the grapevine, she finds out that he is interested in her. One day at lunch, she finally sits down at the table with him. They begin talking and discover they like the same things — skiing, movies, pizza. Wow! It must be love!

Sexual Attraction Is Not Love

Those feelings are so powerful that it would be foolish to try to deny that they exist. The important thing a teenager must realize is that this is *sexual attraction — not love.* A hard concept to get young people to comprehend is that their attractions to members of the opposite sex are physical and emotional reactions in which their feelings and bodies have taken over.

Teens should be told this is a natural feeling. It is natural for men and women to be attracted to each other. There is nothing wrong with it — if it is not confused with love. But love is the unselfish giving of yourself to other people.

Feelings of inadequacy strongly affect a teenager's outlook on love. Teenagers are subjected to a lot of stress, especially if their parents are divorced or away from home often due to work. When these things happen, teenagers probably are not getting the love and attention they so vitally need from their parents.

Mom and Dad may have many problems of their own. They are too preoccupied to spend time with their teen to find out what is going on in his life, how he is feeling, and whether his needs are being met. Unfortunately, this situation is all too common.

There are many teenagers whose lives are filled with hurt, bitterness, hatred, fear, and loneliness. They do not have enough proper opportunities to give and receive love. Not only are they experiencing emotional upheavals and hurts, but they also are having to deal with their bodies which seem out of control with all the hormonal changes going on.

They feel weird physically, then get hit with a great big "glob" of emotional heartache as well. It is no wonder that when someone their age responds to them with a smile, a soft touch, and some kind words, they fall for it like a ton of bricks. It is double-trouble time then.

Learning How To Handle Feelings

Teenagers must learn how to handle their feelings. For example, many young people are motivated to cling together or to form cliques because they are "uptight" and nervous. They fear what others may think about them. They are afraid they may do something that looks stupid or foolish and become the object of ridicule.

Junior and senior high schools are tough environments. Often, if a student does something out of the ordinary, such as dress differently, comb his or her hair differently, or develop pimples, other students will rip that student apart.

Teenagers can be frighteningly vicious and can say some of the meanest things imaginable.

Fearful teenagers are looking for someone to join forces with for mutual support. If the other teens are as afraid as they are, it does not matter. At least they can talk together and present a united front to the rest of the student body, sort of like "buddies" in a war. Teens want to have someone to hang onto. There is safety in numbers, even just one more person.

Loneliness is another emotion that drives teenagers to do desperate things. Loneliness can cause them to turn to drugs or to a sexual relationship, because their emotional needs are not being met. They are not receiving love at home, but they do not know that becoming involved with other lonely persons will not satisfy them either.

A teenager believes this person with which there is such a strong attraction will make him, or her, happy. That is what they have been trained to believe from popular fiction, movies, and television. However, because both teens have the same incredibly strong needs, they cannot meet each other's needs because they are focused so strongly on their own. The relationship usually comes crashing down as a result.

Teens *can* have their needs met by loving others. They do not have to concentrate all of their desires on boyfriends or girlfriends. But parents and church youth leaders must show them this concept. Teenagers should be taught that loving other people involves spending time with them and talking about values, beliefs, and feelings. That is the only way to real intimacy, real friendship.

Adults, much less teens, cannot build strong relationships by making "small talk," by talking about superficial things such as sports or the current fashions. They must build a network of strong intimate relationships with friends, as well as with family members.

That really is the only way a teenager will be able to have a solid emotional foundation on which to begin a godly dating relationship. We constantly teach and train our young people at church to reach out to people of the same sex and develop friendly relationships. Otherwise, those feelings and desires could drive them to become involved with members of the opposite sex whom they really do not love.

Confidence Makes the Difference

Teenagers who have the least problems with the dating issue, you will find are those who are the most confident.

They are the ones who feel good about themselves. They are dealing with their feelings. They have good relationships with friends of the same sex. They are active in school and church affairs. They are involved with other people. Their spiritual lives are developing. They just enjoy life in general. These teens do not have a lot of problems, because their self-worth is to the level that they can be happy even without girlfriends or boyfriends.

Those who have low self-worth feel they just have to have someone else to make them happy. If you have a teenager, and it seems they have a new boyfriend or girlfriend every week, or if they are only thirteen or fourteen and say they are "in love," you need to help develop their feelings of self-worth.

However, it is not going to help for you to say:

"I know why you have all of these friends. It is because you feel badly about yourself, and I am not going to have this anymore. I am going to help you feel good about yourself."

That will not work. You have to *love* them, be kind to them, build up their self-esteem, and develop confidence in them by causing them to feel loved. Otherwise, you are going to have rebellion on your hands. It will be parents versus teenager or teenagers, and you will lose that kind of war.

Helping them is hard work, but the alternative is much too costly to overlook this kind of problem.

Another reason teenagers want to date is because of the fun involved. They just like to go out and talk. Who does not like to be special to someone? Who does not like to be number one in someone's eyes? Also, dating is "cool" and makes you seem popular. Most teenagers think someone is weird if he does not date, especially by the time he is sixteen or seventeen.

I have found the most effective strategy is to get teens to want the *right* kind of relationship, not to try and get them to forget about dating until they are grown up. This way, parents are advocates who are working with them toward a desired goal, instead of adversaries. If parents work as partners to help teens shape the right attitudes toward the selection of a mate, I believe not much wrong will happen.

In the following chapter, I have presented a brief plan parents and teenagers can follow in determining the readiness of a teen to begin a dating relationship.

14

Determining
Readiness for Dating

There are five main guidelines that I have found invaluable in determining a teen's readiness for dating.

1. Is his, or her, relationship right with God and the number-one priority?

2. Is his, or her, relationship with the parents in accordance with the Word of God?

3. Has he, or she, been responsible with school work and other responsibilities?

4. Has he, or she, been responsible with friends?

5. Is he, or she, involved in a local church?

Relationships With God and With Parents

But seek ye first the kingdom of God and His righteousness; and all these things shall be added unto you.
Matthew 6:33

Children, obey your parents in the Lord: for this is right.
Ephesians 6:1

This means the teenager is concerned with serving and pleasing God in everything he does. In this condition, teens will not become involved with people who might distract them from their first priority. Neither would they allow any relationship, good or bad, to jeopardize their walk with the Lord.

Honor thy father and mother; which is the first commandment with promise,

That it may be well with thee, and thou mayest live long on the earth.

Ephesians 6:2,3

A mature teen will honestly recognize his temptations, weaknesses, and inexperience regarding relationships. This will cause him, or her, to listen to what parents have to say. Even if what his parents require seems unreasonable, a spiritually mature teen will listen.

As a matter of fact, if a teen gripes, complains, argues, becomes sarcastic, or pouts, he certainly is not moving his parents toward the revelation that he is indeed ready for a dating relationship.

A mature teen will demonstrate that he is ready to date by thoughtfully pondering his parents' counsel and guidelines and diplomatically discussing differences with them. In a situation where a strong difference of opinion exists, a mature teen will seek for a wise and objective mediator, such as a youth worker or parent of another teen that his own parents may be open to discuss the situation with.

In our own home, Judi and I had very strict guidelines for our daughter. As Christina grew into her teen years, she began to like different boys at different times. Our first step was really smart! We forbade it. How do you forbid someone from liking someone else? Obviously you cannot.

So when we realized through much discussion with our daughter how much turmoil and conflict she felt through really liking someone but loving us and wanting to obey, we saw the foolishness of our actions. We then told her that it was okay to "like" someone, but we began to stress what was appropriate behavior and what was not. We discussed what spiritually mature people do and what immature people do.

Immature teens write "Mary + Billy = True Love 4ever"! Immature teens send messages through other people to tell someone something. For example:

"Will you tell John that I think he is really cute? But don't let him know that I told you to tell him."

Those are elementary school "games." They are not healthy, maturing attitudes toward the opposite sex. We talked to our daughter in a manner that implied, "You have too much dignity and maturity to act so silly." That strategy worked fairly well.

Parents never should reinforce these silly games kids play because they think they are cute. What they are doing with approval is instilling in their child an immature approach to a part of his life that probably will be the most important for several years. Instead, parents should help teens approach this age with maturity.

As our daughter moved toward more serious involvement in dating and relationships, she was not afraid to approach us about dating, and she still is not. She knows we will listen, examine what we believe, look at the situation in question, talk to others about it if necessary, then be honest with her.

She understands our position about dating. She understands that she holds the keys to independence and freedom in her dating opportunities. Her demonstration of maturity and respect tell us what she is ready for and what she is not.

Attitude to Responsibilities

I always say there is no greater responsibility a teenager will have than dating and developing a relationship with someone of the opposite sex. Here are some of the reasons for that statement:

- The relationship may lead to marriage someday.

• The sexual temptations involved with those relationships and the seriousness of the scars that may be inflicted. Temptations include curiosity, the physical drive, peer pressure, familiarity — the more intimate the relationship, the more comfortable a couple can become with touching one another, which can open the door for other things.

• The power of emotional involvement. It feels so good to have somebody special and someone to whom you are special. But this is not the foundation of a solid relationship, which makes this nearly intoxicating characteristic extremely dangerous.

• The maturity required to carry on a long-term relationship with all of its responsibility without losing track of other priorities.

For these reasons and many others, it would be wrong for parents to allow their teenager to handle a dating relationship when he has not shown much faithfulness in lesser responsibilities such as school work. As I said before, if a teen is flunking out of school, there is not much doubt that he also will fail in relationships.

I have asked hundreds of teens if they think it is their parents' responsibility to do all they can to keep them sexually pure until marriage and also guide them emotionally in relationships, and the answer always is a resounding *yes*!

Responsible Attitude to Friends

Trust, giving and receiving love, open communication, and development of numerous fulfilling interactions are traits to take into a dating relationship. Too many emotional problems crop up, and too much arguing and fighting go on, if the person has not learned the basics of interpersonal relationships.

Often you will see couples who cannot seem to stop touching one another. Then there are couples continually in strife because of the time one spends with other people and not with the partner. Either relationship is off-balance and not realistic. Both show lack of responsibility.

Jealousy, bickering, and constant turmoil are signs of a person who has not yet learned to have a mature relationship with a friend. No one was created to receive all of their love, companionship, and joy in life from one person. If you try to do this, it will suck the life right out of the relationship.

Every teen should be strong and responsible in his friendships before an attempt is made at more intimate relationships.

A few years back, our daughter became friends with some teens who at the time were showing very little commitment to the Christian life. We saw her being influenced by them in a negative way. She became uninvolved at church or at school (there but not there), and she developed a complaining attitude about school activities and other things. At the time, it seemed minor and the things we saw were not serious, but we did not like the trend we saw developing.

Therefore, we told her that before she would get the freedom to date, we had to have confidence that she would be influencing others, not them influencing her. Whether she made a conscious decision or not, I still do not know. But a change began slowly to take place in her attitudes. We helped, with suggestions of how to take control of various situations; however, it seemed most of all her motivation was a determination in her heart to change and become responsible.

I may not know her motives, but I do know the results! She began to help some of those same teens come out of a mediocre Christian life by being their leader in a variety of situations. In academics, athletics, being involved in ministry teams — Bible study, missions, and drama — and in integrity, she began to set the pace.

Her friends became the winners and champions every parent likes to see their child involved with. She did not leave her old friends but moved into a leadership role when with them. It was a transformation that has been truly amazing and truly a blessing to us and to her.

Parents, I would advise you first of all to set the example with your own friendships. Be involved with winners. Be sure to talk to your teens about all of this, and let them have opportunities to build friendships and make changes. Get them, or give them, the counsel they need to do this, because this area of life is a huge challenge. They need guidance, encouragement, and motivation.

Being Involved in a Local Church

Psalm 92:13 says:

> **Those that be planted in the house of the Lord shall flourish in the courts of our God.**

Again, parents must set the example. However, parents and teens need the support of godly objective input on the development of dating relationships, and there is no better place to find it than in a Bible-believing church.

Setting aside the obvious spiritual reasons a teenager should be in church, mentioned in a later chapter, here are some positive advantages in relationships that both teenagers and parents will gain from attending church regularly:

• Positive counsel about dating.

• Positive friendships that will exert positive peer pressure.

• Positive teaching and instruction on how to build and maintain godly relationships.

• Positive peer groups from which singles can select potential mates.

A Final Point

Any person considered as a potential date by your teenager, or by you for your teenager, *also must fulfill points one through five!*

Parents must get through to teenagers that they deserve nothing but the best. Then, parents must get their teenagers into the condition where they will be able to attract the best and hang onto the best.

The "best" is not a matter of physical appeal, but a matter of self-worth and self-esteem. If you teach your child to think like a winner and to hang around with winners, they will be winners. (Prov. 23:7; 13:20.) Winners are not attracted to losers.

Parents should go over the steps of this plan with their child or children to see if they disagree. Most do not, in my experience. Most parents usually are able to get any teenager who wants to live for God in agreement with this plan.

Parents need to re-examine the plan with their teen on a regular basis as a reminder and as a motivation for change.

Even if the teen is not a Christian, the parents' responsibility remains the same! They need to give their child freedom based on performance of responsibilities, giving teens a part in determining their own destiny.

Once all these prerequisite conditions are met, I recommend a few other guidelines as well, some of which I touched on in the last chapter.

• I recommend group activities as the initial form of dating. This promotes the friendship factor and limits the romance factor to a certain degree.

• If the couple has demonstrated maturity and openness to the point where they are ready for dating on their own, I recommend staying out of intimate private situations where the flesh can go wild: parked cars, apartments, bedrooms, and other places of intimacy. If a couple needs to be alone to talk, I recommend a restaurant or a public park in the daytime, a place where behavior is restricted by the presence of other people.

A good rule is to teach your teen to never do anything in private that he would not do in public. If your teen is not comfortable "making out" with someone else watching, then he should not be doing it alone. Christians are the temple of the Holy Spirit, so in reality, they are never alone anyway. If they are not comfortable knowing God is watching them do whatever it is, then they should not be doing it.

The question that often comes up in teen groups is this: "Well, how far *can* you go?"

I always respond, "How far do you want the relationship to go?"

Then I advise them in this manner:

"If a couple wants to go all the way to marriage, then they should not be spoiling that marriage by experimenting with the physical relationship. You should be seeing what you need to do to keep the relationship right and growing until you can get married.

"If you really love the other person, you are not going to try to see how far you can go with them sexually. You will want to help them grow up so he or she will be a suitable marriage partner for you. It is selfish to say, 'I like this physical feeling. I like this sexual feeling. I want to satisfy it.' That is lust. It is not giving for the benefit of the other person, and that is what love is.

"If you truly love this person, you will keep your hands off them. You will not be on every date seeing how far you can push things without going 'too far.' If you love this person, you will not sneak around and do things that might bring shame and guilt to both of you. There is no love involved with guilt and shame. In a relationship that has slipped into illicit sex, the foundation is very weak and unless it changes, it will eventually crumble — or even worse — an unwanted pregnancy and/or a forced marriage will result."

The commitment not to be involved with lust is the same commitment required *after* marriage. Teens who learn to deny the flesh and walk uprightly are forming patterns of godly living that will remain with them throughout their lives. If there was little or no commitment to control sexual desires before marriage, there will be great difficulty in keeping their minds from wandering and fantasizing about others after marriage.

The message in the physical relationship is to *go slow.* If the relationship is meant to be permanent, then there is a lot of time to wait, which in itself is difficult. If it does not turn out to be permanent, then teens do not need the emotional devastation that comes when physical relationships occur out of order and then break up.

How far is too far?

I believe holding hands and "light" kissing should be the limit for older teenage couples. For couples over eighteen, I tell them to let the Holy Spirit be their guide — but anything that promotes lust is out of the will of God.

Paul instructed Timothy, who was anything but a womanizer, to **flee youthful lusts** (2 Tim. 2:22). If this man of God needed that instruction, surely it is applicable to all others in an even greater way — particularly in our society with its great emphasis on the physical body and on sex.

No one can trust the flesh: *no one!*

Other scriptures concerning sexual behavior are First Corinthians 6:18-20, First Thessalonians 4:1-7, James 1: 14-16, and First Peter 2:11.

15

Discipline Is Correction

At a trial I once observed, the prosecuting attorney told the judge a ten-year jail sentence would be so good for the defendant because he could get occupational training and be involved in their social reform programs.

The judge interrupted, "Mr. Prosecutor, will you please sit down? You know as well as I do that prison is not designed to help people. It is meant as a punishment, and that is exactly what this man deserves. He has been making automatic weapons and is a menace to society! He needs to be kept off the streets to keep him from killing someone. So quit going on about trying to help him!"

The judge was right. It was not the Court's responsibility to help that guy, but to protect the public from a criminal maniac. Punishment is a way of preventing people from hurting others.

However, parents are not judges or prosecutors.

Their responsibility is to help their children for the future by correction and training, not by punishing for the past. Proverbs 29:15 says:

> **The rod and reproof give wisdom: but a child left to himself bringeth his mother to shame. But the rod of correction shall drive it** (the "foolishness" mentioned in Prov. 22:15) **far from him.**

The only way to have discipline in the home is for parents to be in control — not children!

Some children discover they can control their parents with temper tantrums, nagging, or begging. By the time

101

those children are teenagers, their parents have been trained to give in after a certain amount of screaming and arguing.

Rather than put up with the fuss, Mom and Dad just relinquish any pretense at control and let the teenager have or do whatever he wants. If parents want to be effective disciplinarians, they must refrain from surrendering their authority in the home.

When a teenager is in charge, it is a sad situation. Deep down in his heart, he wants his parents to be in charge. He may never admit it, and probably does not even realize it consciously, but a child knows intuitively that he is not ready to take on the world and make major decisions in his life.

Teens are in a growth stage where they are beginning to make more independent decisions, but they still need the security of having parents to lean on and be the ultimate authority. Teenagers crave independence while at the same time still needing the safety, peace, and comfort that can only come from parental guidance and direction.

Even if there are skirmishes between parents and teens over making decisions, teenagers should not be cut loose to "do their own thing."

The *rod* represents physical correction while *reproof* means verbal correction.

A child cannot be left alone to make his own decisions and run his own life, because that is when disasters occur. Just because his friends get to do whatever they want does not mean he should have the same freedom.

Also, it is a miserable feeling for a teen to think his parents do not care enough to bother correcting him when he needs it. Discipline is the parents' expression of love and concern for their teen's well-being and development.

"Preacher's Kids"

Preachers' children, especially, have a reputation for bad behavior. That tendency goes back thousands of years! First

Samuel 2 relates the story of the sons of Eli, the head priest. His sons behaved terribly. They would "hustle" women for sex at the door of the tabernacle while their father was inside offering up the sacrifices. The high priest's sons!

Also, they confiscated the best portions of the animal sacrifices for their dinners. They were doing evil things, and what is worse, Eli knew it. God dealt with Eli because, although he was doing a great and wonderful job in the house of the Lord, he was doing a terrible job in his first responsibility of being in control of his own household.

As First Timothy 3:5 asks:

> For if a man know not how to rule his own house, how shall he take care of the church of God?

In Eli's case, God finally pronounced judgment on his family life.

> For I have told him that I will judge his house for ever for the iniquity which he knoweth; because his sons made themselves vile, and he restrained them not.
>
> 1 Samuel 3:13

As Eli refused to take authority over his sons and demand that they change, God judged not only Eli and his sons, but all of their posterity. We can be very grateful that today we live under the New Covenant.

Parents cannot force their teens to change inner thoughts and beliefs, but they can restrain them from acting out negative behavior. If teenagers refuse to be obedient after discipline in love and after parents have followed all of the godly counsel that can be obtained, then it is time for those teens to leave their homes.

That is exactly what Eli should have done with his wayward sons. If he had restrained them, Eli would not have suffered God's judgment, and he might have been able to get his sons straightened out for good. Back in those Old Covenant times, Eli could have had his sons stoned for their rebellious and ungodly conduct, as we saw from Deuteronomy 21:18-21, quoted earlier in this book.

In addition to providing materially for their children, it is the parents' obligation to keep their children under subjection to the Word of God. Discipline suited to the individual child's personality is the only way to train children to live according to the spirit instead of the flesh. Psalm 127:3 says:

> **Lo, children are an heritage of the Lord: and the fruit of the womb is his reward.**

In reality, it is the Lord's children that parents are raising because they eventually grow up and leave the parents' home. They always will be related by blood, but mom and dad no longer will be responsible.

Obedience to Parents Brings Obedience to God

As eternal beings, however, those children always are God's concern. In order for children to grow up in the fear and admonition of the Lord, parents must show them how to be attuned to God so they can hear and follow Him. If a teenager refuses to obey his earthly Father, whom he can see, then he certainly will not obey his heavenly Father, whom he cannot see. That is why it is important not to let children continue in rebellion against parental authority.

This does *not* mean that parents should be tyrants, who "lord it" over their teens or treat them like slaves. But they should insist on obedience and respectful attitudes toward themselves.

There are many parents today who do not know how to handle their teenagers anymore. The first thing they need to do is *regain control of the home*! When parents are confident of their authority, they will be able to deal with any behavior regardless of how intimidating it may appear. It is their responsibility to be in control.

Parents need to ask themselves just how bad they are going to let things get in their homes before they finally decide that enough is enough. The longer they procrastinate, the harder it will be to regain control. I will present some practical methods of discipline later in this book.

However, in a situation where parents have been out of control for a long time, they may have to use some pretty drastic measures to take the reins back from that teenager.

After every other discipline has been applied and the rebellion and negative behavior continues, they may even have to say, "You either obey us or hit the road."

Parents must be willing to operate in "tough love" in order to regain authority over their home.

I know of several instances where teenagers chose to leave home after their parents had to give this ultimatum; however, it turned out to be the best and kindest thing the parents had ever done for their teens.

As a teenager, the pastor of our church, Casey Treat, had a serious drug problem and was in and out of jail. Finally his parents had enough of bailing him out of jail and covering for his poor choices. He called one day after having been arrested again. His father's reply was, "Son, you got yourself in there, and this time you're going to have to get yourself out." And he hung up the phone. This was the first time Casey realized he was responsible for his actions and he would suffer the consequences of poor choices. Shortly after this he went into a drug rehabilitation center and became a Christian. He has been living that way ever since.

In another situation, the parents gave a young man the choice of moving out with their finanacial support with certain stipulations or leave and be totally on his own. The main stipulation was to see a counselor (who happened to be Casey Treat), on a regular basis. They paid his rent and provided a certain amount of other financial support. He accepted although he did not enjoy the stipulations. As a result after a period of time, he became a Christian. He has been married now for over 8 years, has four children, is very active in the church and is doing wonderfully.

A very heart wrenching thing for a parent to do, but if there is nothing else which can be done, it is obligatory for the parent to have control regardless of how it feels.

The Lord chastens His children whom He loves, so we should follow that example and correct our children whom we love.

> **Furthermore we have had fathers of our flesh which corrected us, and we gave them reverence: shall we not much rather be in subjection unto the Father of spirits, and live?**
> **Hebrews 12:9**

Discipline Brings Respect

Teenagers will have reverence or respect for their parents for disciplining them, when it is done in an appropriate and godly way. Parents who allow teenagers to do whatever they please will not earn their respect. The above verse in Hebrews goes along with Proverbs 28:23:

> **He that rebuketh a man afterwards shall find more favour than he that flattereth with the tongue.**

Teenagers respect adults who will tell them when they are behaving badly or have a rotten attitude.

Family and friends who say, "Whatever you feel like doing is all right with me," are not helping teens to become responsible adults. The reason many parents do not discipline their teenagers can be found in the first part of Hebrews 12:11:

> **Now no chastening for the present seemeth to be joyous, but grievous.**

When problems arise, it seems so much easier to rationalize, "Oh, he will grow out of it. Let's just let it go this time so he will quiet down."

That attitude is especially common when there are a lot of people around, or when the young person really wants to argue and act rebellious. Giving him what he wants is much easier than confrontation. When some signs point to the fact that something "fishy" may be going on, many parents prefer to believe the best and back off instead of dealing with the issue.

Confrontation is not comfortable — but it is better than allowing a teenager to ruin his life.

I know from personal experience how easy it is to fall into this trap. As a father, there were times when I did not follow my instinct that my daughter's behavior needed to be dealt with. I knew something was not quite right, but I did not want to deal with an emotional and possibly explosive situation.

I would back off from dealing with her and comfort myself by thinking, "Well, if something is going on, it will come up sooner or later."

The problem always did surface, but it would have been easier to deal with if I had nipped it in the bud in the beginning.

Children try to control Mom and Dad from the minute they are born. As soon as they begin talking, they pick up words like "no" and "mine," which they use to control the people around them. Even babies only one-year-old have learned this. If parents do not show their child they are in charge from the very beginning, they will allow that child to develop habits of disobedience and rebellion that will only grow worse year after year.

Children are actually searching for the security that somebody bigger than themselves is in charge of their lives. The rebellion comes out of the insecurity and is a result of their selfish, authority-challenging behavior not being handled correctly.

Parents who wait until their child becomes a teen before they start correcting him will find themselves in a very nasty situation. Although correcting a child may seem unpleasant at the time, it is nothing compared to the problems that eventually will manifest when there is a lack of discipline.

The second half of Hebrews 12:11 says:

Nevertheless afterward it yieldeth the peaceable fruit of righteousness unto them which are exercised thereby.

It is not a joyful occasion when parents must confront their children and/or spank them because they have lied, stolen, or been defiant. However, joy and peace are the results of discipline. Once they have been disciplined, then they can repent and change whatever attitude or behavior prompted the correction.

Then the family can be restored to harmony and even be closer and more loving than before. It is unresolved problems that disrupt the atmosphere of the home.

When our daughter was four years old, an incident occurred when she absolutely refused to obey a direction. Judi and I were not angry or upset. We just had a serious talk with Christina about her misbehaving. When we told her she was to be spanked for her disobedience, she began to furiously squirm, fight, and kick. But she got spanked anyway.

Then I told her, "That spanking was correction for disobedience. Now, you are going to get another one because you rebelled against us spanking you!"

That was difficult for us, but she had reached a point in her development when she had to know for certain who was in control. There was a dramatic change in her attitude and behavior after her spankings. Within five minutes, her tears had dried, and she was happy and excited. This impressed upon me how true the scriptures are. Children do want their parents to be in control of their behavior.

Fathers, provoke not your children [to anger], lest they be discouraged.

Colossians 3:21

16

Ways of Disciplining

A rule book cannot be written for every little thing that will come up, but the major rules should be established before any infractions occur. This will ensure that the children receive the same treatment from either parent. The parents already know what has been decided upon, so they are consistent in their disciplining. Any method of discipline depends on consistency in both parents to be effective.

Once parents have established their authority in the family, they must be consistent in their rules and discipline and in agreement with one another.

Amos 3:3 asks:

Can two walk together, except they be agreed?

Consistency requires deciding what misbehaviors do children get spanked for? What do they get put on restriction for, and at what age? Parents must discuss these issues ahead of time and come to a mutual decision, at least for the major things.

Teenagers are smart. They know when parents are not in agreement, so they will go to whichever parent will let them have their own way and bypass the other.

A friend told me that one day she realized that her sons always went to their father when they wanted to do "fun" things, but they came to her whenever they needed something done, something fixed, or something to eat. Her sons had figured out what they could get from each parent. The same thing applies to discipline. Teenagers know which parent will correct them and which will be apt to let them do whatever they please.

Judi and I decided a long time ago to always talk to each other before dealing with our child, if we were not sure what the other would do. Sometimes this meant having to wait before making a decision. However, usually we can go immediately to the other one and come to an agreement about how to handle a disciplinary problem. This takes extra effort, but it does ensure that decisions and discipline remain consistent.

> **And if a house be divided against itself, that house cannot stand.**
>
> **Mark 3:25**

Fathers and mothers need to be in agreement, but children also need to be in agreement with their parents!

A Divided Household

Children who refuse to obey divide the household. If an entire family is in danger of falling simply because one person is out of agreement, then that one person should be removed. Here again, this is in drastic situations where risk to other children is involved (crime, drugs, etc.), and every other measure conceivable has been employed. For example all the following steps have been taken but still have not brought results.

It would be incredibly hard for a parent to tell the child to leave, as we discussed in the last chapter, but it may be better than losing the entire household.

Rules are established and consequences spelled out. Communication has increased. More attention and love has been given. Encouragement as well as correction is plentiful. Objective input has been received by parents. Qualified counselors have been sought for parents and children. Agreements concerning expectations have been established. Perhaps the teen has stayed with another relative or some significant adult like a youth pastor to give everyone some time and space to think, pray, and examine the situation and themselves.

This drastic of a step should never be taken without having the counsel of a qualified Christian counselor such as a trained Pastor or a Christian counselor recommended by a Pastor.

This type of action or even discussion of this type of action should never be done when the parents are emotionally upset. It should never be used as a threat. It should be presented by the parents after much prayer, counsel has been received, and mother and father are in agreement and in control of their emotions. Screaming out this threat or ultimatum in the middle of a disagreement will communicate to the teenager that he is being punished because the parents can't stand his behavior. The message needs to be: "We love you too much to allow you to live the way you are in our house, and you refuse to change your behavior or accept our discipline. This lets us know that you have chosen to leave our home. Therefore this is the next choice we are giving you. . . ." Then options of different living arrangements could be discussed.

One rebellious teenager can cause a lot of fighting and hatred between parents. Younger siblings also are negatively affected by watching an older brother or sister cause chaos, get into drugs or drinking, and take up all their parents' attention. After a while, the young children begin to wonder why the teenager gets more attention for being bad than they do for being good!

In order to be consistent in the way they discipline, parents must make sure that their decisions and actions do not depend on how they feel at any particular moment. Sometimes parents will *feel* like dealing with a child's behavior, and at other times, that will be the last thing they want to do. Being a parent can be hard work!

Discipline Must Not Depend on Feelings

Suppose one child runs to a parent and complains that a brother or sister is picking on him. A favorite response of many parents is, "Well, you tell them to knock it off!" But that is really a lazy way to deal with a situation and a real "cop-out." Instead of relaying messages, the parent should get up and deal with whatever is happening.

The problem is that many parents just do not want to be bothered or do not want to be distracted from whatever they are doing, such as watching a favorite television program. To maintain consistency, however, parents must deal with children the same way all of the time, regardless of how they feel, then the effort will produce good rewards.

Parents should believe for and expect the best behavior from their teen, but be prepared for the worst. Foolishness in the heart of a child (Prov. 22:15) will surface in all sorts of forms, so parents should be prepared to deal with it.

If you think good church-going teenagers will not steal, you had better think again! They are just as prone to foolish acts as worldly teenagers. That does not mean they are evil or terrible. It simply means they have a sin nature like everyone else. Parents should praise the Lord when children do act foolish at a young age, because that gives the parents a better idea of what form of foolishness that child is prone to and an opportunity to draw it out of them.

Children whose parents are always on them like a hawk never get a chance to act on the foolishness that is part of the immature nature. By the teen years, they have missed out on some important experiences and training, and they will act out their foolishness where parents cannot see them.

That is one reason some preachers' children do get into so much trouble. Too much repression and being trained to worry about what other people think causes them to be determined to act the way they want when they are away from mom and dad.

The times a child acts foolishly are tremendous opportunities to draw that negativity out of his life. This is the parent's chance to train him, discipline him, and correct him for the future.

They should not just say, "Oh, you little brat," and then punish him because he did the wrong thing. That is the world's way of dealing with a child's foolishness. Discipline is meant to be correction that will help the child not only do right in the future but will help him want to do right.

Two Great Tools of Discipline

A parent has two great tools, or ways, to correct a teenager. The first is adding work and the second is removing privileges. Restricting privileges can be very effective; however, a teenager may not always get much incentive to change his behavior from this because he can find other things to do around the house. Using restriction as a disciplinary measure over and over will only bore a teen more than it will change him.

A good alternative is to put him to work. Instead of giving him a week of restriction, make him stay home one Friday or Saturday night (the usual "play" nights) and clean out cupboards, wax floors, clean the garage, or clean the basement. Have him work twelve or fourteen hours (not all at once), and teach him how to have a good attitude while doing it.

Do not let him mope around with a bad attitude, gripe, or complain. The teen earned this correction, so he had better learn the lesson, smile, and have a good attitude about it. Not only will the parents have an opportunity to deal with his behavior, but the teen will learn how to work, and the house will get cleaned.

In many schools if a student misbehaves, the correction method is to have him write, "I will not do such-and-such a thing" over and over again, sometimes hundreds of times. Usually, however, instead of thinking about what he did wrong as his teacher intended, the student is wondering if it would be quicker to write each individual word to the end of the page or to write the complete sentence each time! Most students will not get anything out of that exercise.

At our church school, the student who misbehaves must write a paper on what the Bible says about his behavior or attitude, because it does not do any good to have him repeatedly write something like, "I will not rebel." That is simply a form of punishment.

We have found it much more effective to have a teenager write a paper about what the Bible says is wrong with rebellion and what is right about obedience. This method of discipline requires the student to study the scriptures and to think about the consequences of his behavior.

Parents also can use report writing as a way to deal with a son or daughter's behavior. Have the teen do some research about how his behavior will affect his life.

Removing privileges requires knowing the things that are most important to the teenager and then taking them away for a period of time. Perhaps it is his stereo, television, video game, or playing with friends. Parents should remember, however, that long-term restrictions do not make a great impact on a teen.

If you put a teenager, on a month-long restriction, by the end of the first week, he will have pretty much forgotten the purpose of the restriction and just be waiting out the time. In other words, it will be a punishment instead of a correction. Parents should use restrictions only on a short-term basis.

If you put a teenager on restriction from his favorite activity, do not let him do anything else. Just keep him at home. Through this, he will learn quickly whatever it is mom and dad are trying to impress upon him, and then everyone can move on quickly. Also remember that when he is on restriction, one or both parents also may be restricted! Restriction can be tough on the whole family.

What About "the Rod of Correction"?

The Bible talks about the "the rod of correction" a number of places, as we have seen particularly in Proverbs 22:15. The Word is not talking about a "spiritual" rod, as some people teach, but a literal *rod,* not a belt or a whip or anything like that, but a "rod" or a paddle.

Now there is a place God intended for the paddle to be used, and that is the only place on a child's body that should be disciplined. Parents should never hit a child in the face or use their hands to spank him. The child should only be struck with a rod on the bottom. It will not damage him in any way if it is used properly and not with undue force, but it *will* sting.

Children will not forget how a spanking feels. Spanking is an effective disciplinary tool. One seventeen-year-old member of my youth group stayed out one night until 4 a.m. — when he was supposed to be home by 11 p.m. — without letting his mother know where he was.

I told him, "If you were my son and came home at 4 a.m. after not calling to explain why you were late, you would be bending over for me to lay some 'swats' on you, young man!"

I did not say that because I was angry but because this was a serious thing. What was his mother to think when he was gone for five hours in the middle of the night? No one, not even adults, should have this kind of disregard for another's feelings. A husband should not do that to his wife, and vice versa.

There were three alternatives this boy's mother could consider: He was doing something he should not be doing, he had been injured or worse, or he did not care enough about her to call. I felt he needed his seat of correction set on fire! He would think twice about doing that again.

It was not a matter of being angry with him but bringing him to realize the seriousness of his offense and applying some training to prevent him from repeating it. I believe even teenagers should be spanked for drastic misbehaviors, girls as well as boys. Usually parents find that when they spank an older child, they do not have to repeat it very often.

Spankings should be reserved for only very serious offenses, such as rebellion, direct defiance, lying, stealing, swearing, and cheating. There also is a time in teenagers' lives when spanking brings more humiliation than it does correction. At this point, it is better to use other types of discipline.

In our home our daughter was not spanked after the age of 14. In the years of 12 to 14 the spankings were very infrequent. Before this age they were more frequent. I believe spanking a teenager, a girl in particular, would be a very rare occurrence with special circumstances.

Restricting privileges, adding work, writing reports, and spankings are just some basic tools parents can use in disciplining. There are many other methods parents may find that work as well or better, depending on their child's personality and the particular situation. Parents should seek the Lord on how to best deal with their teen's behavior. Also, as in other situations, godly counsel always helps.

A common occurrence is with poor grades. What I have seen be effective from a parent's perspective as well as from a teacher's perspective is requiring the student to fill out an assignment sheet on a daily basis and having the teacher sign it each day. Teenagers hate to do this and are generally very motivated to get out of having to do it.

If the same behavior occurs repeatedly, they need to search for new ideas and ways of dealing with their teenager in order to take care of the problem. Another thing that can affect how parents raise a child is the situation where one parent is a believer and the other is not. There may be strife and disagreement between the husband and wife, in this case.

The unbeliever may want to listen to rock and roll music or watch R-rated films, while the believer is trying to get the Word into the teenager and get him involved in a Christian lifestyle. Being miles apart like this can cause a lot of problems.

In order to be successful, the believer should first of all be confident in his authority as a child of God. If the Christian will live according to God-given authority, the unbelieving spouse may not like it but will *usually* accept it.

A woman who whines because her husband will not let her train their teenagers in a Christian lifestyle will never make any headway toward resolving the problem. Most of the time, just walking in spiritual authority will change the situation.

If the unbeliever remains adamantly opposed to raising up the children to be godly, then the believer should back off in some areas rather than cause more strife and division in the home. What that mother can do is let her love and example win the child for God and allow the child to see the difference between the fruit of a good lifestyle and an evil one.

Areas Christian parents cannot back off from, however, are the inflexible standards we talked about concerning alcohol and drug abuses, sexual conduct, or criminal behavior. Those are activities not to be tolerated under any circumstances. The born again parent *must* take charge in these situations and absolutely refuse to allow children to be involved with them. There will be no peace in the heart of the believer until she, or he, does this.

If the unbeliever does not think there is anything wrong with a child taking drugs, the believing parent must put his, or her, foot down and deal with the behavior regardless of consequences.

Christian parents will have to decide for themselves exactly what the inflexible categories are, but I do not see how anyone can ever excuse allowing their children to do things that can destroy their lives. I have known some parents who allowed their teenage sons to sleep with their girlfriends right at home and engage in sex. There is no way a Christian parent could feel right about that.

Other issues such as listening to rock and roll music, staying out late, or going to movies will call for more flexibility.

In summarizing this chapter on discipline, the most important thing to remember is that a teenager should hear a lot more positive statements and comments made to him than negative ones. A teenager should receive many more affirmations than corrections. The fact of the matter is that there is a lot more good about teenagers than there is bad. The conversations with them should reflect that.

Epilogue

The concepts concerning the raising of teenagers are never ending. In no way do I intend to imply that the guidelines given in this book are exhaustive or comprehensive. There is so much more that could be said and so many topics that were not discussed.

The main idea I wanted to convey is that rearing teenagers can be done with peace, fun, and success.

In closing, let me sum up a few points:

1. *Treat your teenagers with respect.* Teenagers have great ideas and creative minds. They are no longer "kids" — although their behavior may be childish at times. The more you treat them as courteously as you would an adult and the more you listen carefully to their ideas and input, the more mature they will become. This would include the way you correct your teenager. If you correct a teenager in anger, they will rebel because they identify your anger as disgust and as punishment rather than correction. Remember how you like to be corrected — with dignity and respect. Your teenager deserves the same treatment.

2. *Create fun in your home with your teenager.* Spend both time and money on having fun together. Parents and children need to play together. Plan some activities and ask your family for ideas on what to do. Ask others for ideas, then do something together!

3. *Spend time talking with your teen.* Make sure all your conversations with your teenager and with the rest of your family do not center around problems. Statistics show that teenagers spend an average of seven minutes a week in meaningful conversation with their parents. Make sure your

family does not fit the norm. Plan the conversations and schedule the time for them, or they will not happen.

The principal of our church school, who is a friend of mine with two wonderful teenagers, says his family's best times of discussion about plans, dreams, visions, and activities occur while lying on their bed, just sort of "hanging out."

There absolutely must be a plan for those times. I call it "planned spontaneity."

Often around bedtime, the time of reflecting, some good things come out in talk. As a parent, listening to children at that time will give you a real education! After school or after work also is a good time as well, because children are often ready to share what happened during the day.

However, you must know something about their world to be able to ask relevant questions to "prime the pump" of conversation. Know something about their friends, classes, events, and activities, as well as their interests, talents, and weaknesses. Then you will be able to ask relevant questions that do not lead to a discussion of problems.

4. *Let your children see they hold the keys to the rate at which they receive new-found freedoms and privileges.* Explain the concept of "regulated independence" to them and remind them of it at every available opportunity. Do not use the concept as a club to beat them or a punishment to threaten them with. Use it as a demonstration of appreciation and rewards for faithfulness and good handling of responsibilities. In this way, you will have a tremendous motivational tool to use.

5. *Set an example in your own personal growth.* Parents often have difficulty with teenagers because the parents do not see the teenagers advancing in maturity. This often can be a direct result of what is happening with the parents. It may be that teenagers are not growing because they are modeling

the behavior of the parents. Also, it may be that the parents do not see the growth of the teenagers because they are blinded by the lack of growth themselves. It is difficult to see growth in those close to you, if you are not growing yourself.

If you are looking for things your teenager needs to change, you will find plenty! However, if you are looking for growth in your teenager, you will see it if you are a person involved with growth in your own life. If you reward growth through encouragement and added privileges, more growth will occur.

Apply these principles and watch what the Lord and your teenager will do!

Bob Smith is youth pastor at Christian Faith Center in Seattle, Washington, where the senior pastor is author-teacher, Casey Treat. Bob oversees the entire youth department which ministers weekly to more than fifteen hundred young people in the nursery, children's church, junior and senior high school groups, and young adult's ministry. Also, he pastors a youth group of more than three hundred teenagers, which hosts mission trips, local youth crusades, and a juvenile hall ministry.

Bob has developed a genuine love and concern for young people through both his contact with them and his own personal testimony. Because of his strong desire to reach young people for Jesus and to train youth workers, Bob Smith has dedicated his life to youth ministry.

As a teenager, Bob was destroying himself with drugs and alcohol. At the age of twenty, he entered a drug rehabilitation center, where he was born again and filled with the Holy Spirit. There he met his future wife, Judi, and future pastor, Casey Treat. After graduating from the program in 1974, Bob and Judi were married. Then he went on to earn a degree in social work from the University of Washington. He was named youth pastor after Casey Treat founded Christian Faith Center in 1980.

Bob and Judi are pastors and founders of Christian Faith Childcare Center and Christian Faith School, which is pre-kindergarten through twelfth grade. Founded in 1984, the school now has one of the largest Christian education enrollments in the Pacific Northwest.

Bob has ministered to teenagers and youth workers across the United States, Canada, England, Korea, and the Philippines. He is a popular speaker best known for his practical Bible teaching. He teaches young people to reject mediocrity and to be bold and aggressive in their Christian life. As a man not satisfied with "lukewarm Christianity," Bob shares his message with teenagers, inspiring them to be the successful, world-changing people God created them to be.

The national *Youth Alive Conference* held the second week of August each summer since 1985 also was founded by Bob and Judi. Hundreds of teenagers and youth workers attend each year to receive teaching, training, and inspiration from the Smiths and their personal guests, who have included Russ Taff, Carman, Winkie Pratney, and Blaine Bartel.

Another ministry founded by Bob Smith is *Lightforce International*, a group of singers and musicians ranging in age from sixteen to twenty-six years. This group spends the summer traveling in the United States, Canada, and abroad to minister in contemporary Christian music and in praise and worship.

*   *   *

To contact Bob Smith
write:

Christian Faith Center
P. O. Box 98800
Seattle, WA 98198

Additional copies of
Raising Teenagers Hassle Free
are available at your local bookstore,
or by writing:

Harrison House
P. O. Box 35035
Tulsa, OK 74153